Best Wishes
Pixie Farthing 2022.

NOTHING STAYS THE SAME

Pixie Farthing

Jimmer Publishing

NOTHING STAYS THE SAME

Pixie Farthing

Jimmer Publishing

First published in Great Britain in 2022 by Jimmer Publishing
Copyright © 2022 Pixie Farthing

Pixie Farthing has asserted her moral rights to be identified as the author

A CIP Catalogue of this book is available from the British Library
ISBN 978-0-9556404-1-4

First edition

Illustrations by James Weaver

Designed and typeset in Sabon by Will Weaver

Printed and bound in Great Britain by Biddles Ltd, King's Lynn, Norfolk

With love to the memory of my dear husband Alan who sadly passed away during the writing of this book.

With love also to:

Our five children
James, Sophie, Kim, Vicky and Will

Our grandchildren
Jenny, Holly, Charlotte, Chloe, Jack,
Georgina, Dudley, Peggy and Eliza

And our great grandchildren
Harry, Holly, Amelia, Jacob, Marnie, Teddy and Grace.

C O N T E N T S

ACKNOWLEDGEMENTS

To my son Will Weaver for the design and layout of the book, to my son James Weaver for the use of his original illustrations, to Stephen Rice for typing my handwritten manuscripts, to Julia Stannard for the editing, to my daughter Sophie Weaver for co-ordinating the whole project.

All photographs are supplied by the author with the exception of:

CHAPTER 1: *James Ross Chemist*
From the Mersea Museum/Brian Jay collection

CHAPTER 3: *Victa boat*
From the Mersea Museum/Pauline Winch collection

CHAPTER 5: *Strood railings broken*
From the Mersea Museum/Rose and Len Harvey collection

CHAPTER 10: *Pixie's Rag Trade*
From the Barry Weaver collection

CHAPTER 11: *John Whiting's house/coal truck*
From the Mersea Museum/David Cooper collection

CHAPTER 12: *Old chemist, Barfield Road*
From the Mersea Museum/Jack Botham collection

Chemist new premises 1970s
From the Mersea Museum/Len Rampling collection

FOREWORD

After the success of my first book, From When I Can Remember, I knew I had to continue my story and bring it up to date, but at the same time, be able to return back to some more of the history of the island.

I want to thank everyone who gave me their consent to use some of their tales and activities of the past, ensuring the island history is not lost or forgotten. I hope this book, Nothing Stays The Same, will be an interesting and enjoyable read about life on Mersea.

CHAPTER 1

A visit to the hospital

MILITARY HOSPITAL, COLCHESTER

OVERLEAF: *James Ross Pharmacy.*
ABOVE: *Military hospital.*

The shock of losing my father, Peter, when I was seven months pregnant seemed all too much for me to cope with. It wasn't long after his funeral that I began to feel unwell.

I sat waiting nervously at the surgery to see Doctor Jones. The waiting room was filling up with patients who, after leaving their names with the receptionist, joined the orderly queue of people sitting on the rows of hard, wooden chairs. There wasn't an appointment system; everyone simply waited patiently until it was their turn to be seen. I began counting how many people there were in front of me and hoped they would not take too long.

Deep down, I knew that in all probability I would have to go into hospital. Lucy, the district nurse, had called at the house the day before to give me my weekly check up and she wasn't at all happy with the result. I had promised to go and see the doctor in the morning and continue to have plenty of rest.

The door opened and I knew it was my turn to walk along the corridor into the consulting room. I tapped gingerly on the door before entering. Doctor Jones sat behind his desk.

"Good morning, Ann."

He never called me Pixie – always sticking to the names on the records.

"Good morning, doctor. Nurse Hulbert suggested that I should call in to see you today."

"Yes; she did have a word with me first thing."

After taking my blood pressure, listening to the baby's

heartbeat and testing my water sample, he sat back in his chair and said,

"Well now, I think the best place for you to be at the moment would be in hospital."

"Do I have to go?" I asked quietly.

"Yes, you need complete bed rest for a few days. Get your blood pressure down and then it's possible you'll be able to come home again."

I walked out of the surgery with my mind in turmoil. Why did everything have to go wrong? Feeling close to tears and as big as an elephant, I got on my bike and rode the short distance down Melrose Road. Bambrough and Ross, the chemist shop in Barfield Road, was facing me. I could call in and buy all the toiletries I needed to take to the hospital.

As I opened the door of the chemist shop, there was the pleasant familiar smell of the various products on sale, from medications in the dispensary to cosmetics, soaps and perfumes. There were even veterinary and horticultural preparations and still more, all displayed in cabinets and on long shelves. The shop window had an attractive display to entice the customers.

Mr Ross, the pharmacist, a tall, large-built man was in the dispensary wearing his immaculate white overalls. I stood watching him mix and shake up a bottle of medicine and remembered a day a long time ago.

I was a very young girl. Mum had sent me to buy some Dr White's feminine towels. I was expecting one of the female assistants to serve me, but unfortunately Mr Ross came to the counter and said,

"Hello Pixie. What can I get for you today?"

I was horrified and said,

"Can I have a toothbrush, please?"

"What colour would you like?"

"Blue, please."

Needless to say, Mum was not amused when I returned

home with a toothbrush instead of the required product.

With my mind returning to the present, I purchased the items required for what I hoped would be a short stay in hospital. I was one of the lucky civilians who had been given the option of giving birth at Colchester Military Hospital. Doctor Jones had been off work for a few weeks and Doctor O'Reiley came from the Military Hospital to support Mersea Island. The hospital's reputation was good and we were honoured to be able to have our babies there.

I arrived back home very close to tears and told Mum what the doctor had said.

"Never mind, dear. You've got to do what's right for you and the baby."

I still had a horrible anxious feeling about going into hospital.

I went next door to use their telephone. I didn't feel like going to the telephone box down the bottom of Victory Road, but I needed to let my husband Alan know how I had got on at the doctor's. I phoned him at work and he was far less anxious than I was, telling me to calm down. He said he could be home by mid-afternoon. Our young son, James, would be coming home from school with Mrs French, her daughter (Rachel) and another child called Jackie Hulbert, so I knew I did not have to worry about him.

Mrs French and her family lived a very short distance from us. Our back garden ran from the corner of Victory Road and stretched about three hundred and fifty feet down the unmade track of Rosebank Road, ending opposite to where the French family lived. At the end of the garden lived Jackie Hulbert's family. James, Rachel and Jackie were all roughly the same age and went to West Mersea County Primary School together.

We all had large gardens with plenty of room for the children to play, but they still enjoyed playing in the road. It was considered to be safe. The only traffic would be from the few residents who owned cars, the early morning milkman and

Peter Vince, who delivered the bread in the baker's van. After a heavy downpour of rain, there were large puddles in the road, which were deep enough for toy boats to be launched and often a little paddle in the muddy water would be had.

I could just hear the sound of the children's voices outside as they arrived home from school, then the sound of the back door shutting. James hurried into the sitting room. He looked at me and said in a very grown-up manner for his six years,

"Are you feeling alright, Mummy?"

"Yes dear, I'm fine, thank you. The doctor wants me to go into hospital for a couple of days to rest, but it won't be long before I'm home again. I'll be leaving as soon as daddy gets home from work."

I was trying to be as casual as possible, but could feel an uncontrollable shakiness in my voice. I was sure James knew I was upset. He put his arms round my neck and gave me a huge cuddle.

"I'll be fine here with Nanny – don't worry about us."

It wasn't long before Alan came in from work and my suitcase was put in the car. I knew it was nearly time for us to leave. Sitting in the front of our black Volkswagen Beetle, which had taken us on our adventurous holiday to Spain only a few months ago, I was now going off for some rest in hospital. I knew my mood was pathetic and that I had to pull myself together and cheer up, so I waved happily to James and Mum as they saw us off at the gate.

＊

The Military Hospital stood on the outskirts of the garrison town of Colchester, a twenty minute drive from Mersea Island. We arrived at the large, beautiful Victorian building constructed with fine red bricks and surrounded by vast immaculately kept lawns. There was an impressive portico leading to the main front entrance, with polished wood flooring inside. At reception, we were told that I would be in a ward leading off the maternity ward.

On arrival at the ward, we found the nursing staff were welcoming and friendly. They showed me to my bed and drew the curtains round the cubicle to give me privacy to get undressed. Alan went over to the lounge area where there were comfortable chairs and a television. After the nurse checked my blood pressure, she listened to the baby's heartbeat through a conventional trumpet-shaped instrument (which I now know is called a Pinard Stethoscope). The trumpet-shaped end was put on my bump and the flat end went against her well-trained ear, which could tell if all was well with the unborn baby. I was reassured by her smile, followed by her saying,

"Well that's a strong little heartbeat!"

The nurse pulled back the curtains and said,

"Your husband can take your clothes home."

"Can't I keep my clothes here with me?"

"No, I'm sorry, but we do prefer them to be taken home."

Up until that moment I had been reasonably happy, but now an uneasy feeling swept over me – I wanted to keep my clothes! I suppose it was about me not having any choice. Without my clothes I could not go home, even if I wanted to. Alan was not due back to visit that evening, as I was meant to be having a restful time. This added to my stress. While my blood pressure was being checked again, one of the nurses asked me if I was worried about anything. I replied,

"No, nothing in particular. I just want to go home to my son. I've never left him before."

"You really must try and calm down. You're causing your blood pressure to go up even more."

I tried to relax and read one of the magazines I had brought with me, but I could not seem to concentrate. It wasn't long before the sister came to my bed. With a kind gesture, she held my hand and said,

"My dear girl, I personally think you'll be better off

at home. Hospital isn't the right place for you to be at the moment. You need to be at home with your family, where hopefully you'll calm down."

Within just a few seconds, I became relaxed and a feeling of happiness came over me.

"Can I go home tonight?"

"Providing we can get in touch with your husband."

"If you could phone the next door neighbour, someone will be able to pass on the message."

It wasn't long before a nurse came to tell me that a message had been passed to Mr Weaver and hopefully he would arrive to take me home later that evening. I watched the door expectantly, hoping to see Alan appear. At last he was there, holding the suitcase containing my clothes. A nurse approached him. They appeared to have a short conversation and then he came over to my bed. I couldn't wait to draw the curtains round the bed, so I could get dressed and go home.

"When you're ready, the nurse has a form for you to sign," said Alan.

The form was more or less to say that I was discharging myself and that I was aware of the responsibility I was taking.

"If I sign the form, will I be able to return to the hospital when the baby is due?"

"Yes, of course," reassured the nurse. "It will be on your records that coming into hospital caused your blood pressure to go up even further. However, I must stress how important it is for you to have complete rest when you get home. We have been in touch with Doctor Jones and he has arranged for the district nurse to visit you every day."

"My mother lives with us, so there will be someone there with me all the time."

The nurse smiled and wished me good luck, and hoped she wouldn't see me again until the baby was ready to be born. I was happy and relieved. In only twenty minutes I would be home again.

CHAPTER 1

The main road home to Mersea Island passed The Wick, a huge tract of land, where the army had their main shooting range. The red flag was flying on the tall flag pole. This was a warning signal, prohibiting the public to go across the land while the soldiers were firing live ammunition. The sound of the guns firing was a chilling sound and could be heard as we motored past.

I was glad to leave the sound behind and move a few miles on to Abberton and Langenhoe. These villages are a little confusing. Abberton runs down the right-hand side of the road as you go towards Mersea Island and Langenhoe is on the left-hand side. The Lion pub, although on the Langenhoe side, was always known as *The Abberton Lion*.

The stretch of road from The Lion leading down the hill has always been known as a Roman causeway because it crosses the marshy Pete Tye Common. When we passed Langenhoe School at the bottom of the hill, Alan suddenly began to brake. A herd of cows that had been grazing on the common were crossing over the road at a leisurely pace to get to the grass on the opposite side. Several cars and a bus were all lined up patiently waiting to get past. Time nor tide waits for no one – neither did Mr Nyeman's cows! Our twenty minute journey was without doubt going to be much longer. The baby was kicking away inside me, also wanting the car to start moving.

After the herd had slowly crossed the road, we were able to carry on to Mersea. Mum and James had heard the car arrive and were waiting for us at the door. I had only been away for a matter of hours and it is difficult to describe how happy I felt at being home again. In my mind I knew I was going to do everything I was told. I did not want to go back to the hospital again until the baby was due.

Mum looked pleased to see me, but she had to 'say her bit', as mums do.

A VISIT TO THE HOSPITAL

"You are a daft ha'porth. You know you must rest now that you're at home."

"I know, Mum. I'm going to."

I then saw her soft side as she gave me a kiss.

"Have you had anything to eat?"

"No Mum. I didn't stay long enough to have an evening meal."

"I'll reheat the beef stew and dumplings."

Mum went through to her own kitchen, which was in the old part of the house. It dated back to the 1930s, when it was built by Uncle Will Hewes. I could smell the stew as she carried the pan through. Mum and James had eaten earlier, so Alan and I sat on our own at the table that had already been laid with a clean cloth, salt and pepper, and a butter dish. I reached over for the butter. It was a tradition of the Farthings to cut open the dumplings and spread on a good dollop of butter, which melted down into the gravy to give a delicious, buttery flavour to the good old-fashioned suet dumpling. 'Afters' was a thick creamy rice pud.

I spent the rest of the evening lying on the settee with my feet up, resting my very swollen legs while watching television.

CHAPTER 2

Going to court

OVERLEAF: *'High View' Victory Road.*
ABOVE: *Unmade Rosebank Road, looking south.*

The next few weeks proved to be extremely tedious. There were times when I wanted to be doing something other than being lazy. Mum, at the age of eighty years, was absolutely fantastic. She was still perfectly capable and able to look after everyone, as well as keeping us all in order. I did worry that she might be doing too much, but being busy helped her to overcome the sadness she still felt over the loss of her son, Peter. The past year had not been easy; we were faced with one crisis after another and often we were not sure which way to turn.

It had been rumoured that the rough unmade track of Rosebank Road would be adapted and made up to the standards required for a proper roadway. What a shock we had when the rumours eventually became reality. Everyone received a letter from the council stating the apportionment and estimated cost of five pounds per foot of road frontage owned by each householder! Most of the residents along the road were understandably in agreement with having the road made up, as their properties fronted onto Rosebank Road, with some frontages being as little as thirty-five or forty feet. Our property fronted onto Victory Road, but we were on a corner plot which meant that our back garden ran three hundred and fifty feet along Rosebank Road.

Mrs Hoy, an elderly widow living on the corner plot at the other end of the road, also faced an enormous bill. We were the only two householders who actually decided to object to the road being made up because of the unfair apportionment and excessive costs – our debt would be one thousand, seven hundred and fifty pounds!

Of course, it would have been great to have a proper road, free from the elm trees and hawthorn hedges which grew on top of uneven grass banks running down parts of the centre of the road, but we definitely could not afford it. We sent off an appeal to the Council and eventually received a notice to attend court at Colchester Town Hall. As we couldn't afford to pay a solicitor, Alan had to represent us.

The day arrived for us to attend court. It was a daunting experience with the local council being represented by a QC. Why had we allowed ourselves to believe that we could present a good enough argument for getting at least a reduction in our road charges? After Alan had said all that he possibly could to justify our argument, the judge actually said,

"It does seem unfair, but that's the way that apportionment works. However, may I suggest you sell some land to pay for the charges?"

Alan replied, saying,

"Unfortunately, our land is not considered to be deep enough to conform to the local standards for building."

The judge's reply was,

"Perhaps in these unusual circumstances a more lenient view could be taken regarding the land depth."

The judge had to find for the plaintiff. The QC immediately stood up and claimed for costs. Alan leant over to me and in a whisper said,

"Trumped up little arse!"

Looking directly at Alan, the judge replied,

"Mr Weaver, there will be no costs in this case."

After the outcome of the court hearing, we knew we would have to sell off some land. This proved to be an emotional task for all of us, as the land had once been cultivated by Dad. His greenhouse, which we had still been using, would now have to come down. All the fruit bushes and trees would be lost, but at least we still had our home.

It didn't take long to sell the first building plot to Eric and Diane Fleming, who were going to build their own house. However, no one could ever have predicted what the outcome of selling the second building plot would be. A new land levy tax now meant that we had to pay forty pounds out of every hundred pounds of the selling price, leaving a large debt still owing. We then found out that if we put High View up for sale, we would be exempt from paying any tax. Our solicitor advised us to build a new property on the remaining plot and sell High View. Our family had lived in this house for more than twenty years. It is a terrible feeling when it seems like all your choices are taken away.

I have always felt slightly guilty about employing G.A. Cock and Sons to build our new house because of competitive animosity that used to exist between my late father, Peter J. Farthing, Builder, and Glenny A. Cock, Builder. However, one of the reasons we decided to give the work to them was because we honestly thought they would be able to do quality work and hopefully complete the job quickly.

Any worries or doubts we had about the plans actually being passed by the Council were put aside after Mr Cock arranged a meeting at his home in Yorick Road, West Mersea. He said he couldn't see anything that would stop the plans being passed. Thankfully, the plans for a house and garage at 1 Rosebank Road, West Mersea were passed on the 22nd of April 1968, and the application signed by W.H. Carrington, Clerk to the Council, and E.J. Banner, Surveyor.

CHAPTER 3

Sophia Penelope

OVERLEAF: *Sophia Penelope.*
ABOVE: *'Victa' barge.*

The day had arrived for me to return to the Military Hospital, where arrangements had been made for the baby to be induced. I knew this was the safest option, but no matter how many times I was reassured that all would be well, I still felt a little apprehensive. I was determined to put on a brave face and not worry Mum or young James. Everything was packed in my case and loaded into the car. We were ready to leave. James gave me a big hug, knowing that when I returned he would either have a baby brother or sister. Miss Snell, the elderly lady who lived opposite, was waving goodbye as we drove off.

Motoring off the island, across the Strood causeway which took us to Colchester, the decaying timbers of Victa, a forty-five foot barge that was built way back in 1874, caught my attention. My thoughts went back to the time when the Hewes family lived there, using it as a houseboat. Tragically, the vessel's back had been broken after travelling from Brightlingsea with a full cargo of chalk and stone. It all happened while she was moored across East Hall Channel. The bow was on one side of the channel and the stern on the other. When the tide ebbed she was unsupported in the middle and it broke her back. However, after she was towed into West Mersea, her life was prolonged when she passed a survey to be used as a houseboat. During part of World War Two, she was moored on The Hard. Then, after the war, she was taken to The Shell Works at Peldon by local fisherman, Peter French, where she was first used as a houseboat by the Rowley family. Finally, she finished her time in a small creek on the salt marsh off the Strood, home to the Hewes family.

There was one original deckhouse on the barge, but Cecil Hewes added further accommodation to the deck, which looked somewhat like a shed. This served as a bedroom for his children: Val, Shirley and Catherine. A remarkable sight was seeing Mrs Phyllis Hewes riding her three-wheeled, painted ice cream bike up the long stretch of Wellhouse Hill to Mersea with her children actually sitting in the ice cream box at the front, ready to do their shopping!

As we got further along the road, Alan commented on my silence.

"You're quiet. Are you feeling alright?"

"Yes, I'm fine. I've been thinking about the Hewes family and when they lived on that old boat on the Strood. It must've been hard for them. It was an unusual way of life for the children, but it probably gave them both strange and happy memories."

The road ahead was clear, with very little traffic. Alan was a fast driver, so we arrived early at the Military Hospital. I began to feel nervous as we pulled into the car park. I was booked into the maternity ward and, if all went well, the baby would be born that day. After getting the suitcase from the car, we went straight to the maternity ward. My anxious mood passed as I saw one of my friends walking down the large ward towards me. It was Lil Clarke (née Mills). We had both attended West Mersea County Primary School at the same time, were both living on Mersea Island and here we were greeting each other and discussing babies. Lil had already given birth to her son, who I would be able to see later.

It was strange to hear military ranks used to address the staff here. Sister was Captain, Matron was Major and Principal Matron was Lieutenant Colonel. However, the civilians did tend to use the more familiar terms: Nurse and Sister.

I felt extremely nervous after getting undressed in a side room and putting on the gown I had been issued with. How different everything was to having a baby at home!

After the ungainly procedure of having my waters broken, I really thought I would be going straight into labour. However, as that didn't happen, it was suggested that I put my dressing gown on and return to the ward. I could even walk about, as the gentle exercise would encourage the labour to start. When I got back to the ward, Lil was waiting for me and I was able to see her baby son, who I thought looked like his father, Jim. As we stood talking, I attempted to regain some dignity by trying to hide my enormous bump and hospital gown by pulling my dressing gown together. Lil laughed and said,

"It's a good job you've got your dressing gown on, or you'd be showing your bum! Did you know that the gowns issued here are made by the prisoners at the Military Corrective Camp [The Glasshouse] along the Berechurch Hall Road?"

"No Lil. I didn't know that. You're full of interesting information!"

It wasn't too long before I began to get my first labour pains. Our baby arrived at six o'clock in the evening – a beautiful baby girl. Alan was present at the birth. It is hard to describe the emotion I felt looking at a perfect baby and hearing the sound of that first cry. There had been many ups and downs over the past year – first a miscarriage, followed by the joy of another baby on the way, then toxaemia. Now, I wanted everything to be alright, but I heard a voice saying that the afterbirth wasn't coming away. I had to go to theatre, where the afterbirth would be removed under anaesthetic. I was assured that there was absolutely nothing to worry about – until they were about to push me into the lift. I was panic-stricken and shouted,

"I can't go in there; I won't be able to breathe!"

Alan explained that I had a tendency to be claustrophobic. The nurse was very understanding and explained that it was the only way to get to theatre. She held my hand tightly as I went into the lift. That was the last thing I remember until I was back in the ward at eight o'clock that night – baby in her cot, Alan standing by. It was nearly time for Alan to return home to let James know that he had a baby sister.

The week that I spent in Colchester Military Hospital was a memorable time of good experiences that were contributed to by the fantastic military staff. It was so nice having the dining room separate from the clinical atmosphere of the ward. The table was laid out properly, in the way you would expect in a first-class restaurant, and we were waited on by waiters in their smart uniforms. I enjoyed the experience of socialising at mealtimes with the military wives, together with a few civilians – a variety of people from different backgrounds. It was interesting to listen to the different accents and attitudes, some posh and some not so posh. Posh or poor, we all had one thing in common: we wanted the best for the babies we were soon to take home. One lady already had six children at home, but she still had to prove to the nursing staff that she knew how to bath her baby. We all had to demonstrate that we could bath baby correctly before returning home.

* * *

The day had come for us to go home. Alan had brought the carrycot to the ward the evening before, all ready for Sophia Penelope Weaver. I had to wait until there was an ambulance available, as it was considered the safest way for the baby to travel. When the ambulance eventually arrived, the double doors at the back were opened and I walked up the steps ready to sit on the bench at the side, with the carrycot and sleeping baby placed safely on the floor. The back doors were about to be closed when I felt ever so hemmed in once again.

"Please don't close the doors yet!"

"Why not my dear?" asked the driver.

"What if I want to get out?"

"Well, you only have to say. We'll leave this door open."

He pointed to the sliding door separating the rear of the ambulance from the driver and his assistant. I was more comfortable being able to talk to the ambulance men and we chatted most of the way.

As we arrived home, Mum and her sister, Auntie Tod were both waiting to see Sophia and, as I stepped out of the ambulance, Miss Snell from across the road was waving to us. The baby was carried indoors by one of the ambulance men. James bonded immediately with his baby sister and happily took on the responsibility of being a big brother.

CHAPTER 4

A surprise on
moving day

OVERLEAF: *Nanny Farthing holds Sophia on moving in day.*
ABOVE: *(Top) On the same day, James and Sophia; 'Manana',*
photographed in the early '80s.

Christmas was particularly busy that year – getting used to having the new baby and managing everything that happens during that season. There were some very happy moments, but also some emotional times, especially when thinking of those who were once able to share the festivities, but who had now moved into the heavenly realm. Are they able to watch over us? I would really like to think that in some magical way they can.

As we approached 1969, we were beginning to feel more hopeful that a buyer would be found for High View. A few weeks later, a retired pharmacist, who owned a chemist shop in Watford, contacted the island's estate agent to make an appointment to view the property. As we still didn't have a telephone, Mr Hines, who owned the estate agency in the High Street, came and saw us in his lunch break to arrange a convenient time for the viewing. We agreed that the weekend would be a suitable time for everyone. We were lucky as the Cowings liked the house and were cash buyers. They made an offer, which we decided to accept, of just under the asking price of five thousand pounds.

The day we moved from Victory Road to Rosebank Road was the 2nd of May 1969. It was my birthday and a day I'll never forget. There were tears and laughter, and even a bit of anger to add to the many moods surrounding us all.

We had some really helpful neighbours, Eric Fleming and Peter Hulbert, who were there to give us a hand with the move when we needed them. The furniture only had to be taken a matter of yards (or metres if we use today's measurements).

One piece of furniture to be moved was the sideboard, which was one of my favourite pieces. Peter was going to help Alan move it. There was only one place for it to go and if it didn't fit I would have to get rid of it. Peter and I went with the tape measure to make sure my reckoning was correct. It was going to be a really tight fit, with the sideboard extending slightly over the architrave that went round the door. I knew that Alan did not like this piece of furniture, but it was something that had been in the family since we were at Cross Farm. He would have preferred a more modern style, but this was Edwardian. It was solid mahogany and would probably last another century. Even after the massive mirrored shelf was removed from the back of the sideboard base, it was still very heavy. However, the struggle of moving it into the lounge paid off. It fitted with no room to spare. I had won! The sideboard looked as if it really owned that space.

Alan looked at me, laughed and said,

"Well mate, you've got your way."

The sideboard remains there to this day.

* * *

Mum's bedroom furniture was also going to be moved. It was a very elegant Edwardian set with everything matching, including a dressing table, which stood on long inlaid legs and tiny wheels. There were two long drawers, which were empty apart from the lining paper in the bottom. Alan pulled out the top drawer and carried it on his head. As soon as he walked up the path to the front door, Mum greeted him with what I thought was an unnecessary challenge.

"What on earth do you think you're doing with that drawer?"

"What does it look like? I'm moving it for you!"

"Well, be careful the lining paper doesn't fall out."

"If it does, it can soon be picked up," said Alan.

"That's quite enough of your cheek, thank you!" retorted Mum.

At this point, I felt it necessary to enquire as to what was going on and why Mum was so agitated over something so trivial. Mum replied, saying,

"It's not trivial at all. I've got a little bit of money saved up and it's tucked under the paper in that drawer."

I quickly lifted up the paper to check that her 'little bit of money' really was still there. I could not believe my eyes at the amount that was tucked away.

"Mum, do you know how much there is?"

"No dear, not really. I just save a little when I can."

We went indoors and together we counted the money. There was four hundred pounds!

While we completed the remainder of the move, Mum sat in the living room nursing the baby. I knew she must have been feeling unsettled about everything. We were finding reminders of the past – things of Dad's (Jim Farthing). It was also only eight months since Peter, her only son, had passed away. Each time I went back into High View, I felt sad about leaving the past, but happy for a fresh beginning.

* * *

The day had been long and stressful. The bedrooms were tidy, with the furniture now in place, but the beds still had to be made up. Mum insisted that she wanted to make her own bed. We were still using eiderdowns and bedspreads, as duvets hadn't yet become fashionable.

We were lucky to have a laundry on the island and all the bed linen and tablecloths had been collected, laundered and returned by Ivan King (Ikie) the van driver. Ruth and Lesley Reynolds first purchased the laundry in July 1955. Before that, it had been owned by Mrs Hamilton. It was very run-down at the time of purchase, but employed five people, including a van driver.

After a hard struggle, the trade began to increase and was

helped by the twenty-six large ships that were laid up in The Blackwater Estuary because of lack of trading and the Suez Canal crisis. They had begun to arrive in about 1956/57. The ships were visible from The Hard and along the shore, making a weird and unusual sight for both locals and visitors to the area. There had been times over the years when as many as forty ships were moored in the estuary.

Every day, various goods and commodities were transported to and from the ships by Mike Lungley in a boat called The Sceptre, which was owned by Clarke and Carter who were acting as the shipping agents. A lot of the local traders seemed to benefit from these worrying times. Eventually, the laundry began to prosper and was able to employ many more people who were living on Mersea Island.

My gratitude extends to the Mersea Electric Laundry, especially at the end of the day we moved house as I undid the large, brown paper parcel securely tied with string. Our crisply starched white sheets and pillowcases were all ready for making our beds.

CHAPTER 4

CHAPTER 5

A terrible accident

OVERLEAF: *The notorious crash blackspot on The Strood.*
ABOVE: *Mick Weaver.*

It was the end of September 1969 when Alan's brother, Mick, paid us an early morning visit. This was unusual, particularly as he had been working late the night before – Mick was a very talented musician and had been playing in a band.

As he approached the Strood causeway that linked Mersea Island to the mainland, he could see there had been a terrible accident and one of the two cars had crashed straight through the wooden fencing beside the road, plunging into the mud about five yards from the embankment. Mick made his way home to Barfield Road, unaware of the sinister ordeal which was soon to present itself to his family.

Mick had not been home long, when there was a knock on the front door. His mother went to see who could be at the door in the early hours of the morning. Like most mums, she found it difficult to go to bed until everyone was home. Two policemen stood there and were invited indoors. The news they came with was not good. Margaret (Margie), the youngest of the seven Weavers, was in one of the crashed cars that Mick had passed on the Strood earlier and she had been injured. There were five people in the car and they were all thrown from the vehicle on impact. Fortunately, there was a low tide at the time – another two and a half hours and they would certainly have drowned. Helpers arriving on the scene were able to keep the unconscious casualties from suffocating in the mud. Sadly, one of the young passengers died before he reached the hospital.

It is hard to describe the emotions and feelings that affect the mind and body when you hear such terrible news. At that moment, all we could do was comfort each other with words. It was Alan and Mick's little sister and I could see and feel their sadness. Hopefully, my words of comfort and positive encouragement were some help. Then, hot drinks, biscuits and a game with James and Sophia raised the gloomy mood to something more cheerful.

I am pleased to say that within a few weeks, despite her injuries, Margie made a full recovery.

CHAPTER 5

Kimberley Ann

OVERLEAF: *A fry-up to keep Pixie going, hands full with newborn Kimberley Ann.*
ABOVE: *(Top) Kimberley with her cousin Cindy Benns; Kimberley takes some refreshment.*

We had all got used to living in our new home and an awareness of summer was all around us. The school was preparing for sports day and fruits were on the trees and bushes. I hadn't been feeling too well lately. Usually, this feeling would wear off as soon as I decided that 'I would be alright' – probably no more than a bit of stress.

It was time to meet James from school. As I approached the end of the road, pushing the large coach-built pram with Sophia bouncing up and down inside, James came running towards me, out of breath.

"Mummy, I've got a really funny rhyme to tell you. I didn't want to forget it, so I've been saying it over and over again."

My brother Billy's got a ten foot willy
He showed it to the girl next door
She thought it was a snake
and hit it with a rake
Now, it's only five foot four!

I couldn't help laughing, but did need to tell him that perhaps it was not the sort of rhyme that could be told to elderly aunts and uncles! He would have to be quite wise and thoughtful about whom he recited his rhyme to.

After another week passed, I was still feeling unwell. At times it felt as though I was pregnant, but I thought that was virtually impossible. When I told Alan how I was feeling, he said I should go and see Doctor Jones, as he would be able to put my mind at rest. The visit to the doctor did confirm that as I was still breast feeding the baby and had not had a period since her birth, it was highly unlikely that I was pregnant – not impossible, but quite rare. I was to stop worrying and return if I continued to feel unwell.

When I arrived home, I decided to confide in Mum about going to the doctor and the reason for my visit. Her reply was just what I expected.

"Well young lady, let's hope the doctor is right. If not, you will certainly have your work cut out!"

"I know, Mum. I'm sure he's right."

However, it wasn't long before I just knew I was pregnant. I was feeling sick in the morning and unwell at other times during the day. I had to go back to Doctor Jones' consulting room. When I entered, he looked up, smiled and said his usual thing,

"Hello Ann, what can I do for you today?"

I told him exactly how I was feeling. He appeared surprised, but said it would be necessary for me to leave a sample of my water taken first thing in the morning so that it could be sent to the hospital for a pregnancy test. The result would be back in about a week. There were no home pregnancy tests in those days.

In less than a week, I had heard that my pregnancy test was positive. Yes! I would have two children within eighteen months! It seemed impossible, especially after having to wait six years for Sophia to arrive. I was pleased to be offered the option of returning to the Military Hospital again to have the baby.

The family were surprised to hear that another baby was on the way and a further surprise was the news that my sister, Susan, was also pregnant and would possibly be having her baby at the same time at the Military Hospital, although the exact date for me was difficult to predict, because of the unusual circumstances.

CHAPTER 6

On the 23rd of May 1970, the doctor decided to book me into the hospital for the baby to be induced to avoid any further complications arising. So there we were, parked in the hospital car park and unloading my case from the car, ready to have another baby.

Susan had given birth to her baby the day before. She had decided to take herself to the hospital, as her baby was eight days overdue. She claimed she was having contractions, although the staff at the hospital didn't find too much evidence that she was in labour. However, they decided to induce her and the baby arrived in the afternoon. When I got to the ward, I found I was in the bed next to her. It was lovely having her there beside me.

My baby arrived early in the evening on the 23rd of May. Alan was present at the birth – another beautiful little girl weighing only 6lb 4oz.

Susan left the hospital the day before we did. I felt lost after she had left, but I was intrigued to hear the Military Hospital was supposedly haunted. There had been many strange sightings of a ghostly figure in Victorian nursing uniform. She would walk down the corridor, before suddenly vanishing into thin air. During World War Two, a patient claimed he saw a nurse in old-fashioned nursing clothes changing his bandages. Could she possibly have come back to help her patients? Which corridor did she walk along? Sadly, the Military Hospital was closed in 1977 and was later demolished. I sometimes wonder if the nurse will still find a place to walk.

As I sat waiting for Alan to collect us from the hospital ward, I had time to think about how busy our lives were going to be. The one thing I was absolutely sure of was the incredible bond of love between me and my children. I knew it would last forever.

Alan arrived with the pale yellow carrycot, which once belonged to James, then Sophia, now Kimberley. She looked so tiny and peaceful, all ready for the journey home. When we

KIMBERLEY ANN

got to the car, the carrycot was placed on the back seat. There were no seat belts in those days, but we all arrived home safe and sound and continued to travel in this manner for some considerable time.

The baby had only been home a matter of days and was lying in the carrycot, which was on the stand. I looked down, thinking how peaceful she was and noticed the side of one cheek looked badly swollen. I looked at Sophia, who was standing by the cot with a bag of chocolate Maltesers in her hand. I knew immediately what the lump was and was quickly able to retrieve the melting sweet. There were no real side effects – only to me. I knew at that moment in time that I must never expect anything less than mischief. Anything could happen to my two baby girls if I didn't remain vigilant!

CHAPTER 6

New shoes and a party plan

OVERLEAF: *Alan and Pixie, dressed up for a night out.*
ABOVE: *Alan.*

Although Mum was now eighty-two years old, she was still able to help me with the children. She was always there when I really needed her. However, there were occasions when I felt she was interfering. Of course, I loved her immensely and still wanted her to be around for a long time to come.

Meanwhile, Alan was travelling to Sible Hedingham to work every day for H.J Rawlinson, Corn and Seed Merchants. He worked in the busy office doing general office work, including bookkeeping and typing. Although it was considered to be a well-paid job, there were times when we found it difficult to make the money go round.

There was one time when Alan was invited to attend an evening function with his boss, Peter Rawlinson, as well as a number of colleagues and farmers. The dress for the occasion was dinner jacket and bow tie. Alan did own all the smart gear, but the shoes were getting shabby. I am not sure why, but over time I seemed to have taken over the responsibility for buying his clothes.

I knew it was time for a new pair of smart black shoes, so I went off the island to our nearest town, Colchester, and purchased some very smart fashionable black shoes. I couldn't wait for him to open the shoebox and see them.

At last he saw the shoes, with their long slender toes and the very latest highish heels. He tried them on – they were the right size.

"I don't like these bloody high heels," he grumbled.

"Alan, they're the latest fashion."

NEW SHOES AND A PARTY PLAN

"I don't care if they're the latest fashion. I still don't like the heels."

"I'm sure you'll get used to them."

Alan had been doing some work in the garden shed, when suddenly he burst through the kitchen door with his new shoes in one hand and a hacksaw in the other. I looked at the items he was holding and realised he had tried to reduce the height of the heels with the saw, only to reveal hollow centres. I don't know what annoyed him most – my laughter, or the fact that he had ruined a new pair of shoes!

Once I was on my own, I was able to rescue the situation with Polyfilla. I decided to fill the hollow heels with the white plaster-type cement. Alan wasn't too impressed with the improvised improvement.

"You can't leave it like that with the white showing in the centre of the heels – looks a right bodge up!"

"Don't worry, I can fix it."

I did indeed fix it, with Zebo, a black polish used for cleaning iron stoves. It worked perfectly, thank goodness! If money had not been an issue, he could have bought another new pair of shoes.

Two days later, Alan returned home early from work so that he could be on time for the evening function. The evening went well – until Alan glanced at the carpeted floor and noticed a trail of white Polyfilla. Would anyone realise where it had come from? He sat down discreetly and hoped not!

* * *

The era of the '70s saw big changes in our family. The children were keeping me very busy and growing up fast, but I wanted to make a financial contribution towards paying for our overheads. I was beginning to formulate a plan in my mind where I could perhaps do some 'Party Plan' selling. Alan and Mum both thought I was crazy to even consider such an idea, but I was so convinced that I could make it work that nothing was going to stop me.

There was a firm called Motif Fashions, who designed and manufactured high-class childrenswear. The factory was situated in Brightlingsea, about five miles to the south east of Colchester and the owners were Brian Reynolds and Monty Heslop. I knew Brian very well, as he was a close friend of my brother, Terry.

After talking to Brian and telling him my idea about Party Plan selling, he agreed to let me choose a good selection of their designs and said I could pay for the items after I had done my first party. I had worked out a good profit margin – even with a percentage being given to the person hosting the evening. The first dress party was a complete success, so I was able to pay for my stock and have money to invest in more designer clothes, ready for the next party.

CHAPTER 7

A dodgy knee
and an act of God

OVERLEAF: *Ron Hunt.*
ABOVE: *Mersea Island Football Team, '69-'70.*
From left: (back row) Ron Hunt, D Parkin, R Proctor, A Amos,
B Milgate, J Mackillop, P Roberts; (front row) P McQuoid,
P Sales, Colin Scott, Colin Anstey, D Hempstead, I McDonald.

Alan was also being kept busy with Mersea Island Football Club. He had taken on the job of voluntary club secretary. He came to this decision after seeing Doctor Jones about his knee which had been periodically stopping him from playing football. He was told by the doctor that he should either give up playing or have an operation. It was a hard decision to make – if he had the operation he would be off work for many weeks, which he felt he wouldn't be able to afford to do, but to give up playing football was also very hard. He decided to stop playing competitively, but by being secretary to a very successful club he could still be involved with the game.

Ron Hunt, an ex-professional player with Colchester United Football Club, was now the training coach at Mersea Island Football Club. He had been able to turn Mersea into a successful club that had enough local supporters to need a motor coach to transport them to away games. The Essex Junior Cup Final actually needed three coaches for the supporters. The players for the game were P Roberts, P McQoid, R Proctor, C Anstey, P Sales, B Milgate (captain), C Scott, D McKillop, I Macdonald, D Parkin, D Hempstead and T Saye.

Over the centuries, there have been many strange and spooky tales told about the Strood causeway leading onto the island. Ron was involved in an unexplained experience one Saturday afternoon. He was on his way to Mersea for a very important cup match. As he approached the Strood, he realised the tide was over the road. He felt a sense of panic and despair come over him – how would he get to the match? Then, a thick fog appeared and hovered over the top of the water. Nothing could be seen ahead. There was a ghostly silence, even cutting out the sound of the car engine – yet he seemed to be moving! Suddenly, he was on dry ground and the sound of the car engine brought his mind back to the drive up Wellhouse Hill and the short journey to the Glebe, where the match was to be played.

When his car pulled onto the field, his players were amazed that he had been able to get through the water. It was a particularly high tide and no traffic was getting onto Mersea. Ron was unable to explain how he had crossed the Strood. There were no splashes of water on his car, nor evidence of any other vehicles having been able to get onto the island. Nothing could account for this strange happening. Perhaps it could be said to have been 'an act of God'?

CHAPTER 8

CHAPTER 9

Victoria Ellen

OVERLEAF: *Pixie and baby Victoria.*
ABOVE: *Victoria experiencing a 'wardrobe malfunction'.*

I knew without doubt that there was another baby on the way and the only thing that worried me was telling Mum. When I eventually got round to telling her, the reply was,

"Well, my girl, you've got some hard work ahead of you, that's all I can say."

I didn't pursue the conversation any further and neither did she. I knew she would support me in any way that she could, even if I had to accept a certain amount of criticism.

Being pregnant again didn't necessarily mean I would be unable to continue selling Motif childrenswear. I was enjoying the opportunities for socialising that the parties presented and the money I was earning was very useful. As long as I kept fit and well, I couldn't see any reason why I would need to stop working, especially as I was able to enjoy my time with the children during the day. They always came first. It was hard work, but so rewarding. On the few evenings when I did my clothes party sales, I was able to pay a babysitter out of my profits. Alan was never at home on a Monday evening as he had football club meetings at the British Legion. However, even with the young babysitter, I knew Mum was always around and would be there as back up if there was ever a real emergency.

* * *

The morning had arrived for me to make another visit to the Military Hospital. I had been booked into the maternity ward by my doctor to have the baby induced. It was a procedure I had become accustomed to when having my babies.

Alan left me at the hospital on Saturday morning, the 29th of July 1972, promising he would be back in time for the actual birth. He needed to get some important papers signed regarding a new contract at work. I wasn't unduly worried, as the staff assured us that nothing would happen until the afternoon. He gave me a big hug and kissed me goodbye, assuring me that he would be back very soon.

After changing into the hospital gown and being attended to by the nurse, I was left in a side room to relax and wait to go into labour. There was a bell at hand which I could push if I required the nurse at any time. I lay back on the pillow and decided to unwind and read the book I had brought with me.

I am not sure if it was my relaxed attitude, but it seemed only a short time later when I thought I could feel my first pains. After a while, I decided to push the bell button. It wasn't long before the nurse came and spoke to me.

"Are you feeling alright Mrs Weaver?"

"Yes I'm fine, but I am getting some pains and they're becoming fairly regular."

After the nurse had given me a thorough check, she looked and smiled saying,

"Well, I can confirm you're now in labour."

"Oh, I do hope my husband gets here on time!"

"Of course he will. You still have a long way to go. I'll check you again later."

I lay back on the pillow again and tried to keep calm, but the pains were definitely getting stronger and more frequent. I reached for my bag to get a Polo mint to suck and tried to read some more of my book. I didn't want to make too much fuss, but the contractions were really getting strong and I was getting very uneasy. I decided to ring the bell again.

The same nurse returned, but before she was able to talk, I said breathlessly,

"My pains are very strong and coming very quickly."

She made an immediate check and her reply came fast.

"You need to get to the delivery room right away."

I was helped off the bed and told to be careful as I walked slowly to the room where my baby was to be born. I began to realise it was highly probable that Alan wouldn't be at our baby's birth. Another nurse was also now present and the birth was imminent.

I gave birth to a strong, healthy baby girl weighing 8lbs 8ozs. Alan arrived just moments after, sorry that he wasn't there for the arrival of his beautiful daughter, Victoria Ellen. She really should have been born the previous day on James' tenth birthday. It was the date that Doctor Jones had originally given me to go into hospital, but my reaction was to plead with him,

"Please doctor, it's James' tenth birthday on Friday. Can I wait just one more day?"

He hesitated before giving an answer.

"If you can promise me that you will rest with your feet up, doing absolutely nothing, then I'm sure that it can be arranged, but take care as your health and the baby could be put at risk."

He knew that there were plenty in the family to take care of the birthday party and that I really would do what he said.

James' party went well with a good mix of boys and girls. Even his little sisters, Sophia (or Sophie as she now liked to be called) and Kim, were well behaved and enjoyed themselves.

After thinking about the party and giving birth to the baby, I was now suddenly feeling tired, but still on a high and ready to return to the ward. Alan saw us both settled, me in bed and baby in her cot. He was going home to check on James, Sophie and Kim, who were being looked after by my mum (Ada), Alan's mum (Nanny Weaver) and Auntie Tod. In fact, we were so lucky with friends and neighbours all on call and ready to help if necessary.

* * *

VICTORIA ELLEN

The Military Hospital was still a very special place, once again providing me with the excellent all-round medical care I had experienced during previous stays on the maternity ward. The waiter service at the dining table and choice of good food was all part of helping the patients' recoveries.

Since being there, I had got into a conversation with Elsie Loughlin and her friend Hilda Taylor. Both had been civilians working for the army and were reminiscing on times past. Elsie actually worked at the Military Hospital for a time. She was matron's maid and part of her work was to look after Major Fernleigh's caps which were worn on the wards. She then went to clean at Roman Way Camp, situated off Berechurch Hall Road, Colchester (opposite the Military Corrective Camp). Hilda was already working at Headquarters where the regimental sergeant major was, as well as other high ranked personnel from the Black Watch Regiment.

The two ladies told me a funny story about the day they had just finished polishing the large table in the sergeants' mess and the pipe major, who was a particularly tall man, entered the room, moved across to the table, lifted up his kilt and promptly sat down on the shiny surface. On arising, he had left the imprint of his big arse and anything else that was under his kilt on their beautifully polished surface!

CHAPTER 9

CHAPTER 10

Pixie's Rag Trade

OVERLEAF: *Pixie's Rag Trade in Barfield Road. Many businesses have occupied these premises over the years, including Whiting's and currently, Chez Sally.*

It didn't take long for the family to get used to having another baby in the house. James, Sophie and Kim welcomed her with love and affection, touching her gently on her tiny hands.

I had been led to believe that breast fed babies would have immunity to most infectious illnesses, so I wasn't too worried about the chicken pox that a lot of young people were getting. Unfortunately, it wasn't true as far as baby Victoria was concerned. She was only two weeks old when she developed the disease.

Good old Doctor Jones was able to put my mind at rest, as usual, by saying with a chuckle,

"Don't worry. At least she won't scratch the spots. Use calamine lotion to reduce the irritation and I'll give you something to keep her temperature down, but do let me know if you are at all worried and I'll call in to see her."

Those were the good old days!

* * *

Victoria was now being called Vicky and we were into the new year of 1974. I had got an exciting challenge ahead of me: despite being criticised as being 'mad' by Alan and Mum, I had come to a decision to open a children's clothes shop in Barfield Road. It was once known as The Dairy, owned and run by Mr (Muggy) Mason and his wife. Sadly, Mr Mason had passed away and the shop had been unused for a long time.

After talking to Mrs Mason about renting the little shop,

she became really interested, as she said she would like to see the shop used again. She was living at the back of the premises and it would be less lonely for her. The rent was £5 per week; the equivalent today would be £52 per week.

This was an exciting time for me and I was determined to make the business work, but I knew that I could not allow myself to give less than one hundred percent to the children. They would always have to come first. I knew Alan and Mum had their doubts as to whether I would be able to manage, but I was determined to prove them wrong.

Whenever I had time to myself, I would quietly plan in my mind exactly how I was going to organise my time. I knew I couldn't cope without some help. Sally, my sister-in-law, could help two days a week. Wednesday was half-day closing on the island, with shops closing in the afternoon. It could easily be done with good planning and careful management.

Everything started to fall into place. The decorating was completed; the new deep blue carpet had been fitted, giving the small shop a warm and welcoming atmosphere. A lovely old wooden till stood on the counter. Each time the drawer was opened, a hidden bell inside would ring and the new till roll would turn round. The customer's purchase could then be written down in the small oblong window space, which was edged with brass. Outside, Norman Burgess, the local sign writer, was up a ladder printing the name I had chosen for the shop – Pixie's Rag Trade.

I needed to make a trip to Brightlingsea to get some more stock, ready for the day the shop would open. Brian and Monty now owned what was once the old trouser factory in Western Road. It was the first time I had been to the new premises. I was surprised to see the large, impressive room full of various machines and equipment used to make the fine clothes which they had become known for designing. There were what appeared to be hundreds of rolls of colourful materials and one of the workers was at a large table cutting out the clothes from patterns. There always seemed to be new designs to tempt their buyers and that day I did spend more than I intended!

CHAPTER 11

A *warming drink*

OVERLEAF: *Miss Snell. Neighbour who lived opposite,
on the corner of Rosebank Road, for many years.*
ABOVE: *Whiting's house, opposite Mersea Avenue,
now demolished.*

My boutique opened in January 1974, during the power strikes that had first started in December 1973. We were already being faced with sudden electrical power cuts. There would be no warning and suddenly the whole island would be without electricity. Sometimes it would happen during the day, another time after dark, and every house would be plunged into darkness. There was an eerie look everywhere, with just the light from the odd passing vehicle, or the moon and stars. Slowly, the darkened houses would show signs of light as candles and oil lamps were lit. Kettles and saucepans were being heated over Valor oil stoves, or maybe a Primus heater.

Many people over the years had blocked up their open fireplaces in favour of the modern oil boiler and central heating, but now the oil boilers could not be ignited without electricity. Although we had decided to have the modern and cheaper option of oil-fired central heating, I still also wanted an open fireplace in the lounge. Alan said it was a waste of space and money, but luckily I won the argument. We had an open stone fireplace with a heavy oak mantelpiece. Now, with the frequent power cuts, we were all still able to keep warm by the open fire. Our attic had also become home to what was now proving to be a lot of very useful clutter: Tilly lamps, Valor Stoves, oil heaters and Primus stoves – enough to be able to get by without electricity.

One of the various measures introduced by the Conservative Government to conserve electricity, which was being severely limited by industrial action from the coal miners, first began

A WARMING DRINK

on the 1st of January and lasted until the 7th of March 1974. Commercial users of electricity were restricted to three named consecutive days each week when they were allowed to work, but they could not put in longer hours than their normal day. Services which were deemed essential like hospitals, printers of newspapers and supermarkets were exempt.

During the time of the coal shortage, electricity cuts and all-round austerity, it was a hard time for many people who were in business. However, Mersea Island didn't seem to be affected too badly on the whole. John Whiting, a much respected and well liked local coal merchant, worked during the strike, transporting coal from the boats at The Hythe in Colchester. He used his large trucks to distribute to the outlying districts. Most of the coal coming in on the ships was from Poland and the unloading was done by a company called Fieldgates. It was opencast coal, inferior to our British deep-mined coal, but John was known to secretly leave a bag at the back door of any old people that he felt were struggling to keep themselves warm.

During this cold spell, at about eleven o'clock one morning, there was a loud knock at the front door. I opened the door and standing there was an elderly Gypsy lady. It was not unusual, as we often had Gypsies calling and I never turned them away. They were working in a way that had been passed down through generations. I even believed that there were some who were gifted with possibly being able read the future through looking at the palms of your hands. There had been times when I had passed on some of our unwanted clothes. They knew if they asked, I was either a soft touch or gullible.

This morning, the latter was probably the best word to describe what happened next. The old lady said,

"I'm so cold, my dear. Could you get me a warming drink?"

Knowing there was a bottle left from Christmas, I replied, "What about a glass of sherry?"

"That would surely help an old lady – you're very kind."

I poured her a glass of sherry and before I handed it to her,

CHAPTER 11

she put the two fingers of each hand into her mouth and gave a very loud whistle. I then saw her beckon to some more people up Rosebank Road and five other Gypsies appeared.

"Would you give my friends a drink, please?"

What could I say?

"Yes, of course I will."

I went indoors and poured five more glasses of sherry. I now had six Gypsies at the front door – some were sitting on the doorstep, all drinking sherry out of the best glasses.

Miss Snell, the prim and proper old lady who lived opposite, later came across and knocked on our front door to ask if everything was alright. She wondered who the strange people were on the doorstep and asked if someone had been taken ill. When I told her what had happened, she felt I should be a little more sensitive about who I was entertaining at the front door.

I had never felt threatened by the Gypsies and always tended to buy something from them. However, there was one occasion when I saw some small lace tablecloths in a shop in Colchester, identical to the one that a Gypsy had told me she had crocheted herself in her caravan home. I paid double the price of the one in the shop. I never did say anything to anyone about my expensive lace cloth. Perhaps I paid extra for the 'luck' that came with it? I also learnt that things aren't always what you think they are.

THE BOWLING GREEN
Elmstead Market

Fashion Display
by
"PIXIES RAG TRADE"
West Mersea

Thursday, 22nd August 1974.

8. 15 p. m.   Admission Free.

SNACKS AVAILABLE 20p.   *ALL TAKINGS FOR CHARITY*

CHAPTER 12

A nylon stocking and a bigger shop

OVERLEAF: *Sophie, Kim and Vicky modelling clothes down on The Hard; an advert for one of Pixie's fashion displays.* ABOVE: (Top) *The old chemist; the chemist's new premises in the '70s.*

Barfield Road was a busy main road, with Eastern National buses passing through every half hour. Pixie's Rag Trade had a bus stop directly outside, so apart from customers calling in after meeting their children from school, people getting off the bus would gaze in the window and often come in to look round and have a chat.

It was through having conversations with various people that I began to realise that there was a call for more fashionable adults' clothes on the island. I was seriously thinking I could introduce some ladies' wear, but there was not enough room – it would have to remain a dream, for now. If I had a week when sales were down at the shop, I would get in touch with some of the people who had previously had a dress party in their homes, in the hope that they would book a date with me to sell the latest children's fashions. They would be paid a commission on their sales. This usually worked extremely well.

There was one occasion when I had booked to do a party in Gosfield, near Halstead, Essex. Sally had already worked two days in the shop, but agreed to come with me in the evening. We loaded all the stock which we were taking into the car. I needed to return home first to make sure Alan was there with the children, as Mum was holding the fort until he returned from work. I had already given the children their tea and Alan's dinner was being kept hot on the plate over a saucepan of simmering water covered with a saucepan lid – no microwaves in those days!

He had just returned home and all was well. Seeing us off at the gate, his last words were,

"Have a safe journey. Have you got a torch in the car?"

I confirmed we had everything we needed, including a torch.

The journey to Gosfield was about twenty-five miles, but tonight it seemed to be taking quite a while. It had been a long day. Sally and I had been chatting about anything and everything when I suddenly said,

"Are our lights getting dimmer, or is it my imagination?"

"I think you're right. They are getting dimmer."

This was scary, as we were in the middle of the countryside. It was pitch black and there were no street lights. I began to feel uneasy, but I found myself laughing.

"I'm sure we haven't got far to go."

The lights were getting worse. In fact, I could hardly see the road ahead.

"Sally," I said, "I really can't see where we are going. I daren't stop the engine in case it won't start again!"

The torch was on the floor by Sally's feet. She bent down and picked it up and I stopped the car, taking care to keep the engine running. She opened the door and got out saying,

"I'll walk in front with the torch and lead the way."

We moved slowly along the road. Luck was with us – we could just see a telephone box a few yards along the road. I stayed in the car, frightened to take my foot off the accelerator. Sally was able to telephone the lady who was hosting the party. We had only one corner to turn and we would be at our destination.

On arrival, we unloaded the clothes and dress rails. I introduced us and proceeded with the demonstration, while the man of the house very kindly looked at my car. The bad news was that the fan belt had snapped, however, there was also some good news. He was able to repair it with a nylon stocking and he was confident it would get us home.

The evening went well socially and there were a lot of good

comments made about the stock. However, for the very first time, I did not sell a single item. Perhaps the young mums were caught up with the general financial hard times. There were promises of getting in touch at a later date and some said they would like to visit the shop in Mersea, but there were no sales.

On the way home, Sally and I had a good laugh about the disastrous time we'd had!

* * *

By May 1974, my tiny boutique selling clothes for tots to teenagers had become fairly well known. I was approached by the local newspaper, The Gazette, who asked if they could do an article on the shop and the popular fashions that were now available to young people.

I was delighted with the idea of the publicity and agreed that my daughters, Sophie, Kim and Vicky could model the clothes on West Mersea beach, down by the small boats. The Gazette did a fantastic article, which took up the centre pages and the resulting increase in trade was noticeable.

My idea of wanting to stock ladies' wear, but not having enough room in the shop, could now become a possibility. According to a customer, the property which used to be the chemist shop further down Barfield Road was soon going to become available for rent. The chemist had moved to new larger premises next door.

When I got home that evening, I told Alan what I had heard and that I would like to find out how much the rent would be. His reply did not altogether surprise me.

"Well, it will be too much for you to even think about being able to afford!"

"Unless I ask Mr Morris, I won't know whether I can afford it or not," I responded.

We agreed that I should telephone the next day to find out exactly what the cost would be and if it was affordable.

After talking on the telephone to Mrs Morris, I wasn't altogether fazed by the monthly rent, but it would be one hundred pounds per month more than what I was paying at the present. However, with the extra space and being able to sell the additional adults' clothes, I thought that I could probably make enough profit to cover the additional cost.

I was able to view the shop later in the day. I liked what I saw. I didn't want to lose it and took a gamble. I said yes!

My dream was now becoming a reality. The big new chemist shop was now up and running having been opened by our Mersea doctor, John Llewellyn Jones, BA, MBBS, LRCP, MRCS. I would now be trading next door to a busy and popular pharmacy that was selling a wide variety of cosmetics and toiletries, and also had a licence to sell wines and spirits. The customer potential for me was good. I was sad to leave my boutique, but excited to move into a larger shop at 35a Barfield Road.

After moving, I was lucky to have my loyal workers, Sally Weaver, Pauline Jay and Dorothy Mussett. We all had children, but it worked very well for us, as we were able to adapt our working times whenever necessary. None of us wanted to put work before the children. Another lady called Angela Barclay also became a very handy person to have working for me. I had not known her until she came to the shop and said she would like to get some work on the island. She spoke as though she was a well-organised and efficient person – probably better than me. I decided a little more help in the shop would be good, especially during the holidays, with the children off school.

* * *

I had agreed with licensee, Douglas Brock, to put on a fashion display at The Bowling Green public house at Elmstead Market, a large village not too far from Colchester, on

CHAPTER 12

74

Thursday, the 22nd of August 1974. It was part of the Truman's Festival Weekend. The festival was to be staged around the unveiling of a coat of arms commemorating the tie between Elmstead Market and the de Tany family, who were Sheriffs of Essex and Hertfordshire at one time. The estates in Stapleford and Elmstead were inherited in medieval times. The last of the de Tanys died in the year 1317.

It was hard work for everyone who took part in the show. The right styles were chosen by the models themselves, who all came from the Mersea and Colchester area. I was lucky to have gathered together nine fantastic models who showcased seventy outfits. The night was good and everyone appeared to enjoy themselves. The pub was packed and all from Pixie's Rag Trade were pleased to take part in this celebration.

CHAPTER 13

James gets a job

OVERLEAF: (Left) *Shirley Moore behind the counter at Garnham's, the last of the family to run their business; James proud with his new bike, Miss Snell's bungalow behind him top left.*
ABOVE: (Top) *Looking up The Lane from Coast Road; The Firs during its heyday.*

James was about thirteen years old when he decided that he would like to do a paper round, as he wanted some extra money in his pocket. He left home earlier than usual one morning so that he could call in at Garnham's paper shop in Yorick Road before catching his bus to Stanway School.

As he opened the door, Alec Garnham was sitting on his usual tall chair where he marked up the papers ready for deliveries. Not being a man of many words, he just said,

"Yes?"

James replied politely,

"I was wondering if there are any paper rounds available at the moment?"

Alec knew every round like the back of his hand, so it did not take him long to reply.

"There's only one available at the moment mate and it's in the Coast Road area."

The school bus was due to leave in only a matter of minutes, so James quickly replied.

"That would be ideal for me and I could start straight away."

"I want you here on time, seven days a week. Your wages will be the going rate. You're responsible for keeping your delivery bike in good order and you can start work on Monday. You're the Weaver boy, aren't you?"

"Yes."

James thanked Alec and rushed off to Fountain Corner to catch his school bus, an Osborne's Coach.

The paper round that James had been given wasn't the

easiest, but it was probably the most interesting. One of the properties he delivered to was called The Firs, a beautiful old house situated down Firs Chase. It started originally as a farmhouse built with Tudor bricks and had a thatched roof (probably then called Red Brick Farm).

It has been said that in 1666, the year of the Great Fire of London, the person who then owned the property was entitled to Free Harbour Rights. These were given by King Charles II for the generous act of sending a barge from Mersea Island to London, loaded with a gift of food for poor people who were suffering great hardship because of the fire.

During the eighteenth century, a large extension was added to the front of the building. This gave a very elegant appearance to the grand, eight-bedroomed house, which was once the home of Willoughby J. Bean, a prominent local landowner who eventually lost all his money.

There was a suggestion of the presence of a ghost in the house, which had been talked about for some time. The ghost had been an issue over the years for paperboys; their imaginations seemed to have worked overtime when walking up the long tree-lined driveway. There was talk that they had all heard strange noises and felt uncomfortable when delivering the papers. James did not hang about when he was a paperboy, except on Mothers' Day, when he decided to pick me some daffodils from the enormous display on the lawns under the trees.

The Passodoro family were owners of The Firs and one of their granddaughters, Mafalda Tapp, is (at the time of writing) still living there. I was invited into her beautiful home and felt honoured to see this wonderful piece of history. I was privileged to walk up the grand staircase, visit the eight bedrooms and gaze through the windows at the surrounding gardens and old outbuildings. For years, I had listened to the many tales about The Firs and I asked Mafalda,

"Is there really a secret tunnel?"

CHAPTER 13

Her answer was,

"Yes, but my father had it bricked up to avoid us children venturing into the hidden dangers beyond the secret door." The length of the tunnel or passage, and where it led to, remains a mystery.

I was also told by Mafalda that many years ago during the era of smuggling on the island, the horses in the stables would be removed secretly during the hours of darkness and returned later, sweating and tired. The servants and stable workers kept quiet and they were rewarded with the gift of a full keg of alcohol, left in the stables.

The Lane, which was also part of James' paper round, held many unusual tales and a lot of history. There was a long unmade track that still leads off The Lane, which would have been wide enough to take horses and carts or carriages in the olden days. At one time, this track was called Creek Hall Lane, being named after the property that was once there called Creek Hall. This was replaced in Victorian times by a substantial elegant house named Creek House.

At the end of this lane, stretching nearly out onto the marshes, are three very old cottages believed to be three to four hundred years old. They were probably part of the Hall, or may have been fishermen's cottages. During the dark winter mornings, with a strong wind blowing off the sea and across the marsh, the creaking of the large trees lining either side of the driveway made it a spooky journey for the paperboy.

Today, it is all part of The Lane and all the properties are known by their numbers and not so much by their names.

CHAPTER 14

Sophie goes to hospital

OVERLEAF: *Sophie.*
ABOVE: (Top) *Fashion show adults – from left: Ruth Woodley, Pixie, Susan Benns, Judy Sealey, Angela O'Dell, Kate Fox.*
(Below) *Fashion show children – from left: (back row) Mandy Cockett, Julie Benns, Suzanne Ditchburn, Nick Woodley, James Weaver, Christian Woodley, Shona Morris; (front row) Nicola Frost, unknown, Cindy Benns, Kim Weaver, Sophie Weaver.*

Sophie had shown an interest in wanting to go to dancing classes, her preference being ballet. Liz Clements, the local professional dance teacher, had a studio at her home in Firs Road which was just a short walk from our house. I made a booking for both Sophie and Kim to attend the ballet classes. Sophie loved going, but Kim only went a couple of times and decided not to go any more. Sophie practised and danced around at home, loving to show off in front of people. She could not wait to get to her next lesson.

On one occasion, Liz spoke to me and said,

"I'll be able to turn your little girl into a star one day. She has that special something!"

I felt so pleased, as I knew that was what Sophie wanted. She would say,

"I want to be a dancer, Mummy."

* * *

During the early part of 1974, all our family, except me, became ill with a flu-type virus. Alan was so ill that the doctor had said that if the antibiotics didn't bring his temperature down within forty-eight hours, he may have had to go into hospital. Luckily, the medication worked.

The family all recovered, with the exception of Sophie, who would have a period of being well, then her symptoms would return and she would be ill again. It became very worrying. She eventually ended up in the Military Hospital. The care she received there was really special, but she never seemed to recover fully. Various blood tests were carried out, including a test on her bone marrow. I can still remember the feelings I had waiting for the result of the test that would rule out leukaemia. I remember sitting there – my mouth so dry and my hands sweating. I looked across the ward and the doctor was making his way towards me.

He was able to tell me that they had ruled out the worst scenario, but they still had not found out what the real problem was. He wanted to get Sophie into the Essex County Hospital in Colchester, as they had links to Great Ormond Street Children's Hospital in London. When necessary, paediatricians from London were able to visit Colchester to attend to the young children in hospital. Anything that would make her well again had to be good.

Sophie came home again for a while until arrangements were made for her to go to the Essex County Hospital. She had been there for about two weeks and I spent as much time with her as possible, with Alan calling in every evening after work. Our little girl was beginning to look weak, pale and frightened as blood tests were being taken all the time by the various student doctors. I sat there watching helplessly. I asked one of the students if they were getting anywhere with their tests. Her reply was,

"Well, I'm looking for something unusual – something to do with chickens."

Her reply puzzled me and I wondered if Sophie had picked up some sort of disease when she'd been collecting eggs from the neighbour's chickens.

On one particular afternoon, the doctor treating Sophie came to see her. I asked him if they had found anything. With his hands in his pockets and swaying from his heels to his toes, his answer came in a very posh tone,

"My dear girl, we are still chasing moonbeams."

I was so upset and angry by his reply that I said,

CHAPTER 14

"I'm going to take Sophie home."

"You can't do that," he retorted arrogantly.

"Just watch me!"

I walked out of the ward to the telephone box outside and called Alan to let him know exactly what had happened. He replied saying,

"Calm down and give yourself time to consider the situation before doing anything too drastic."

My reply was,

"Alan, I just know I'm doing the right thing."

Something deep down inside me was suddenly making me feel very calm.

"Alan, she needs to be at home. She's missing the other children and her Nan. She needs building up with some good home-cooked food, and lots of love."

"Well, you really seem to have made your mind up to take her home."

"Yes, Alan, I have, and I know it's for the best and the right thing to do – I must go now, the money is running out."

I went back to the ward. Sophie was resting on her pillow. Her little face was pale and she looked sad.

"Hello my darling. Mummy is going to take you home."

A big smile appeared on her face as she asked, "When, Mummy?"

"In just a little while."

While I was with Sophie, a nurse came and told me the doctor would like to have a talk with me. I was taken to a side room along the corridor, where there were numerous doctors and nurses. There, the intimidation procedure started. The doctor who was in charge of Sophie began threatening to take her into care. He said I was unbalanced and not fit to care for her, and that I did not know what I was doing. Just for a minute, I secretly panicked, but replied calmly,

"I know exactly what I am doing. I am quite capable of looking after Sophie at home. Of course I don't want you to close the door on us. I am quite prepared to bring Sophie back as an outpatient whenever necessary, but I am still going to take her home today."

When I got outside the room, a female Indian registrar, who had always had a kind and gentle manner, approached me and said,

"Mrs Weaver, I personally think that you are doing the right thing. Sophie will recover better at home with her family. She is certainly missing her brother and sisters."

Her kind words gave me the courage I needed to go into the ward and get Sophie.

After arriving back home, there was much excitement as James, Kim and Vicky greeted Sophie. It was a lovely surprise for them. Mum walked into the sitting room, looked at Sophie lying on the sofa and said,
"How are you, my little darling?"

Sophie replied by raising her arms up for a kiss and cuddle.

The next day, we were visited by Doctor Joan Jones. She had received a telephone call from the hospital. They were not happy with me taking Sophie home, but Doctor Jones said she was able to convince them that Sophie would be well cared for and that she would be visiting our home to see her every day.

Sophie began to improve. Her childish laughter could be heard again as she began playing games. James often played Mastermind with her (a code-breaking game, extremely popular in the 1970s, using combinations of small different coloured plastic pegs). The description on the lid says, 'A game of cunning and logic for two players to break the hidden code'. There was an occasion when James admitted he was getting bored, because he said he intuitively knew all the colours Sophie had chosen for the game. This was a strange phenomenon, something we were unable to explain and it only happened when James and Sophie played.

* * *

CHAPTER 14

Sophie's health continued to improve. The colour was beginning to return to her cheeks, but she was still poorly. By October 1974, she was able to take part in a fashion display at West Mersea Yacht Club. I had agreed to raise money for the Royal National Lifeboat Institution by putting on a show with clothes for all ages. I got a team of children together and they were all very entertaining, modelling the outfits as expertly as any professionals. I am sure that all their parents felt the same as I did – very proud. It was a hugely successful evening.

At last, Sophie's illness was diagnosed. After all the various tests over a long period of time, the doctors now knew it to be Still's Disease (also known as Juvenile Arthritis). On a bad day, her joints would be sore, swollen and red, and she would have a high temperature. The treatment was Aspirin and to rest the inflamed joints.

Although it was a distressing time for everyone, we all managed to help Sophie enjoy a fairly normal home life. We adjusted our lives accordingly. Kim and Vicky had been used to playing boisterous games with Sophie, but they were aware that care had to be taken when they all played together now. However, they were all still full of mischief and got into numerous naughty situations. There was always something going on at the 'Weaver's'.

On one particular occasion, there was a loud knock at the front door. It was Mr Whitehead, who lived directly opposite.

"Hello, Mr Whitehead," I said, wondering why he had called.

He answered in his well-spoken accent.

"I say, Pixie, your two little girlies have managed to get your car out into the middle of the road."

"Oh my goodness, how on earth have they managed to do that?"

I ran into the road and could see Kim in the driving seat and Vicky in the passenger seat. I pulled the door open.

"What do you think you're up to, you naughty girls?"

Vicky replied,

"Kim made me!"

Looking into the car, I could see I had left the keys in the ignition. I knew I was partly to blame. I got the car back onto the drive and began to consider what the consequences could have been. It was lucky that Rosebank Road was not a busy place.

CHAPTER 14

CHAPTER 15

The Puppet Theatre

OVERLEAF: *Puppets.*
ABOVE: *Courtneys in the '80s.*

Mersea Post Office allowed people to advertise their unwanted items for sale on postcards, which were displayed in the window for a small charge. Many people would have a quick look for bargains when they posted their letters.

On one particular afternoon, I had a quick look at the adverts and noticed there was a Pelham Puppet Theatre for sale and it included a large variety of Pelham Puppets. James had already got a few puppets, so I immediately became interested and wrote down the phone number.

When I arrived home, I told James about the advert. He was excited and keen for me to ring right away. I hoped it was all still available. On telephoning the number, I was told that Gregory Davis owned the theatre and that he did performances at children's parties with his friend, Clive Ashmore. We knew the Davis family quite well, so we were looking forward to seeing them the next day at their home where we would view the items being sold.

They lived in a nice old house called Courtneys which was approached from Prince Albert Road onto an unmade hill called Hillybrooms. At the top of the hill, there was a turning on the right which led to a long unmade tree-lined driveway. In the mid-1970s, Courtneys stood on its own in the middle of nowhere, but today it is surrounded by houses. It was originally built in 1925 for a Station Master, and then later owned by a retired vicar, Reverend King. After Reverend King, the house became the property of Ralph and Audrey Davis. Today, it is owned by their son, Paul.

When we arrived, we were taken to a room where the Puppet Theatre had been assembled so that we could view everything properly. What a fantastic toy! We loved it and bought the lot.

While chatting, Ralph told me that he had worked as a sales representative for the Western Biscuit Company in 1956. He called regularly at sixteen different grocery-type shops on Mersea Island, selling the firm's products. How times have changed!

We said goodbye and packed the last of the puppets into the rear of the car. Now, James had something to look forward to working with, but if he intended to do children's parties he would need an enthusiastic partner to help with the entertaining. Alan was impressed with our purchase, but did not think much would materialise regarding the entertainment side of things.

Judy Seeley, one of the young people who was frequently at our house, fell in love with the puppets and the whole idea of teaming up with James and entertaining for children's parties. They worked really hard writing their own plays and, after much rehearsing, were ready to perform in a fairly professional capacity. James and Judy were both very competent and confident. Soon, the bookings started to come in and so did the pocket money.

The children attending the parties would get really involved with the acts, participating verbally when it was appropriate. One day, one of the acts had a scene where there was a witch and a skeleton appearing together in a spooky, misty atmosphere. This could be created by using smoke tablets that were purchased from what we knew in those days as The Trick Shop in Eld Lane, Colchester. I'm not sure if Health and Safety law would allow this today. Suddenly, the smoke became rather thick and the children ended up coughing and choking! That was rather embarrassing, but the moment passed and it all finished happily with everyone enjoying the show and party.

CHAPTER 15

It was quite hard work for James and Judy after the puppet shows had finished. The theatre had to be dismantled and all the puppets packed neatly away in their boxes, ready for either me or Alan to transport everything home ready for the next booking.

CHAPTER 16

A birthday poem

OVERLEAF: *The family cuddle up in the big round bed.*
ABOVE: *Alan in one of his many flambouyant 'kipper' ties,
and Pixie.*

Birthdays are a frequent occasion in our large family – this time, it was Alan's. The children were excitedly planning his birthday party and they were each giving him separate presents, which they had chosen themselves.

That evening, before his birthday had arrived and all the presents were wrapped up, Alan had gone off to a football club meeting. I suddenly realised that I had forgotten to get him a birthday card. In a blind panic, I picked up a large piece of white cardboard, which was lying on the table, thinking I could probably paint a picture and make my own card. Then, realising that would take too long, I began to write a poem instead. However, it ended up taking longer than the birthday card would have taken in the first place!

This was written in the 1970s and was found in a box of old papers I was clearing out about a fortnight ago. It made me and the family laugh, so I have decided to include it in this short chapter.

A Poem For Alan's Birthday

Many many years away
Upon a lovely morn
A little boy called Alan
Upon this day was born.
He was very pink and lovely
in every kind of way.

His mother did adore him
more and more each day

Now as he did grow older
He seemed to be more naughty
How could a child so sweet as he
Ever get so dirty?
Alan is growing quickly
How the time does pass
He hasn't long had those new pants
And now he's through the arse.

His poor old Mummy loves him
And tells him to be good
He says Oh yes of course I will
But do you think he would
At five years old he goes to school
To learn his ABC
Although he's still naughty
A bright child he will be

Now he has come up to ten
His knees he wants to hide
His waist is far too skinny
And his trousers far too wide
Alan is a choir boy
A pretty voice has he
But still a little bugger
As he will always be.

The Lord I think has improved him
The devil has done more
But his poor Mum still prays and prays
For what she is not sure
He loves his mother dearly

CHAPTER 16

And does try to be better
A girlfriend would do wonders
If only he had met her

Mother is delighted, a girlfriend home for tea
Perhaps at last he's seen the light
And seen the light has he
Many girls adore him, he likes them all a little
When the right one comes along, that will be the battle
The wedding day at last is set
He's wed the girl that he first met
They've made the vows that they must keep
Further happiness they will seek
To Alan and Pixie a boy is born
A sleepless night and a lovely morn

Time is passing, James is six
Alan and Pixie have been up to more tricks
Baby two is on the way
A sleepless night
A lovely day
Sophia Penelope is one day old
The end of November is very cold
This baby is so very sweet
A better one you'll never meet.

Alan and Pixie have made a mistake
A bun in the oven is starting to bake
Number three will soon be here
Sophia Penelope is only a year
A lot to handle these three will be
There'll not be no more, says Alan, you'll see.

Another sleepless night another lovely morn
Kimberley Ann has now been born

A BIRTHDAY POEM

What a tiny little baby
She will be better when a lady
Now she is nearly three
She is as lovely as can be.

Alan was a randy old bugger
Three was enough
But now he's made another
A family of six is plenty enough
It's earning the money to feed them that's tough.

Another sleepless night the dawn of a new day
Number four is on the way
Oh, what a whopper, it's eight pounds four
Victoria Ellen is a Weaver for sure

Many pleasant moments these children have brought
To Alan and Pixie a lesson is taught
A round bed to sleep in is very delightful
The results of not sleeping
Are not just a trifle
However they must take the rough with the smooth
And hope their financial state will improve
If it doesn't they're in dead lumber
It costs a fortune to feed this number

Happy birthday Alan Dear
Hope this verse will bring good cheer
see you home in bed tonight
Everything will be alright

CHAPTER 17

Business as usual

OVERLEAF: *A new premises on High Street, shown here as the Eastern Electricy shop.*
ABOVE: *Moving premises again – another new shop for Pixie on Church Road.*

Alan did all my bookkeeping for the shop. One evening, after a long session of going through the accounts, with paperwork all over the sitting room, I was asked to check some of the items listed – including wages, stock and rent. After some input from me, he sat back, lit a cigarette and said,

"Well Pix, I'm sorry, but your profits are down. It's not worth all the hours of work that are going into the business."

I could not believe what I had just been told.

"Alan, are you sure? We have lots of customers and the weekly takings are good. I thought everything was going well."

Alan replied, saying,

"It's the high rent that's keeping the profits down."

We spent a long time talking about what could be done. I did not want to work on a higher profit margin by putting up the prices. I could lose my customers that way. We really needed to be able to rent something more affordable, but agreed that for the present time we could stay where we were. We were not losing money, but we were not making any either.

However, it wasn't long before I heard of a property that would possibly soon be available for rent, situated next door to the fish and chip shop in the High Street. It was what used to be the old Eastern Electricity shop, where the locals used to go to pay their electricity bills or purchase electrical goods from the showroom. At the present time, the shop was being used by a Mr Granger to sell second hand and antique items. This was the person who may be able to help me relocate to new premises. I had been told that he was seriously considering the idea of moving on. After talking to him, I was successful with my bid in acquiring the shop, then known as Fortunate Finds. Soon, it would be known as Pixie's Rag Trade.

The property had a history of first being Cherry Tree Cottage, built around the 1880s from wooden boards. During the 1930s, it was owned by a well-known Mersea Island builder, Gilbert Rowley, who lived there with his family and adapted the property slightly to allow for his office. By the late '30s, Gilbert sold the property to Eastern Electricity. I already had in mind what I could do to mix the traditional, old look with today's 'trendy' look.

I believe the property at that time was actually owned by Mr Herbert Bishop, a prolific property owner on the island. I presumed he would be my landlord, but to this day, I still do not know who had the rent payments each month.

Brian Jay and a gentleman called Glen approached me after moving in, asking if they would be able to rent some of the floor space to sell their aqua diving equipment. As their stock did not conflict with anything I was selling, we shook hands on a deal, which worked well for us all.

* * *

I had been trading in the High Street for less than a year, when I noticed one of the shops in Church Road was up for sale. It was situated next door to a bank on one side and launderette and dry cleaners on the other side. It was already a ladies' dress shop, with a lovely big window displaying dresses on mannequins. I felt I simply had to enquire about this property. It would be fantastic to actually own this shop – it had a touch of class about it.

My mind went back to the time I first moved into the High Street. About three shops down the road was a high class ladies' dress shop and next door to that was Len Burton's shop that sold wallpaper, paint and anything to do with home

CHAPTER 17

decorating. It was a lovely day and I had decided to put a couple of rails outside our door to attract customers to look at the stock. Len often used to come and see us for a chat. On this occasion, he came to tell me that the lady from the posh dress shop next door to him had just seen my rails outside and tutted in her up-market accent,

"Oh dear, they are lowering the tone of the place."

Len really made me laugh, mimicking both her walk and her voice.

Against all the odds, luck was on my side and I actually became the owner of the shop that was for sale in Church Road, so I would be moving on again.

* * *

The move was keeping everyone busy, including the people working for me. Poor Mum was not in the best of health, but she was a strong-minded lady and refused to let her illness take over. I think the love she had for the children gave her the extra strength to carry on.

I was lucky to have Angela O'Dell, a hard working teenager, who babysat the children when necessary and worked in the shop all day on Saturdays. There were times when I did have doubts about whether I had done the right thing in purchasing my own shop. It was hard work at the best of times, but now I was pregnant again. I wondered if it would all become too much. I managed to keep everything ticking over, with my family and friends helping where possible.

However, the time came when I had to recognise that the business would have to be sold. Our four children, plus the one on the way, were the most important thing to me and they had to come first. We were also aware that Pixie's Rag Trade had been able to support the children financially, providing them with perhaps a slightly more desirable lifestyle. They had become used to various treats, including designer clothes.

BUSINESS AS USUAL

Sophie had attended ballet classes until she became ill, then piano lessons, which seemed to be an option that would make up for the disappointment of not being able to carry on with her dancing.

On the 3rd of November 1975, Sophie passed her grade one pianoforte. Her teacher at the time was Miss Geoghan, who lived and taught from her bungalow in Mersea Avenue. James also had piano lessons. His teacher was Mrs Allen, who lived in Yorick Road. Kim and Vicky were both younger and were not making any big demands at that time. That would come later!

Although the business was on the market, we still had to carry on trading until the right buyer came along with an acceptable offer. You could say it was 'business as usual'.

CHAPTER 17

CHAPTER 18

Pixie gets towed away

OVERLEAF: *Alan's boat 'Pixie'.*
ABOVE: *In the early 2000s, Alan revisited his Blackwater adventures with a new boat.*

Alan enjoyed fishing in the Blackwater River, just off Mersea Island. On some occasions, he went out with Tony King, Ken Mole and Harold Mole. Ken and Tony had built their boat, named We Two, in the back garden of the old Barfield Road Council Houses, next door to the Weaver's.

One of Alan's wishes was to be able to have his own boat and it was around the mid-seventies that we began to talk about the possibility of it happening. I was always optimistic and thought it was a great idea. Alan liked the thought, but wondered if we could afford it.

It wasn't long before the search started and we looked at both new and second-hand boats. James also showed a big interest. A seventeen foot Mayland Sea Nymph eventually became the favourite and the cheaper version without a cabin was ordered. There was great excitement on the day that the boat was due to arrive.

Sadly, after the boat had been used a few times, it was evident that it was taking in too much water and would have to be replaced with a different boat. It was as though it was meant to be, because Alan suddenly said,

"Bugger it! I'm going for the one with the cabin this time."

So, we now had a lovely fishing boat with a blue cabin that was named Pixie. Because of the cabin, it could also be used as a family pleasure boat. As it was 'moored' in the front garden, Sophie, Kim and Vicky climbed into the boat and the cabin became their play house.

When it was a fishing boat on the Blackwater, there would

be competitions between Alan, James and crew, and Tony King and crew, as to who could catch the most, or the biggest fish. Their catch was usually cod, whiting, flounders, dabs and occasionally, skate.

Our boat had given great pleasure to a lot of people, but she had now been unused for a long time, for various reasons, and it was decided it was time for her to be sold in order to possibly make room for a caravan.

It was a sad day watching Pixie being towed away by her new owners, but, as she moved out of sight, we made a decision that when the time was right there would be another boat. That decision and those comforting words made us feel better.

CHAPTER 18

CHAPTER 19

William Peter

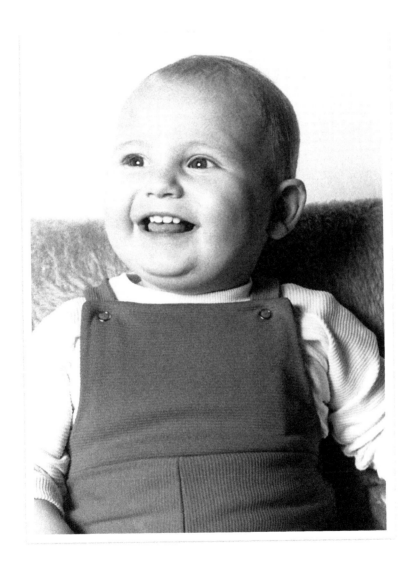

OVERLEAF: *New arrival William Peter.*
ABOVE: *William sits on his big sister Vicky's knee.*

A decision had been made to induce my baby and I had been booked in at Colchester Maternity Hospital, Lexden, for Monday, the 13th of December 1976. On researching the place where my baby would be born, I found out that the hospital, originally known as The Maternity Home, was first opened in 1932 by Doctor Ruth Bensusan-Butt, a General Practitioner specialising in midwifery. By 1935, it had been extended to take twenty patients, with the adjoining house being acquired and used as a nurses' home. By the mid-1970s, there was a special care baby unit that had eleven cots. By this time, the hospital had seventy-nine beds, including forty in the obstetric unit. There were further extensions in the 1980s, but the building still maintained an appealing look of the 1900–1930s.

On arrival, Alan was allowed to park the car on the premises for a specific time, but then had to go and park in one of the side roads. This gave enough time for me to get signed in at reception and settled into Flat 2, which in those days was kept for older Mums – I was thirty-eight years old.

I was probably in the first stages of labour, when suddenly we heard the sounds of police cars and fire engines. It sounded like a big emergency! Alan, sitting at the side of my bed, let go of my hand and said,

"I won't be long, dear. I'm just going to check the car."

"Please don't be too long, Alan."

"I won't be longer than five minutes."

He was quite a bit longer than five minutes, as he was parked next to a car that had caught fire! Luckily, our car was alright and Alan moved it. He returned in plenty of time to see our beautiful son born. It was an easy birth, although he was over 8lbs 4oz – about the same size that James was at birth.

I was allowed to return home after forty-eight hours. I couldn't wait to see the children again. There were only ten days until Christmas Day and I knew there was still a lot of work to be done.

When Alan arrived to take us home, baby William was tucked into his carrycot ready for the car journey to Mersea. The cot was placed on the back seat – this was still considered a safe way for a baby to travel. However, I did squeeze into the back of the car so that I could keep him safe.

As we travelled through Mersea village on the way home, the decorations and lighted trees in the shop windows reminded me how close we were to Christmas and how lucky and poignant it was for the family to have our own Christmas baby.

When I arrived home, I was so pleased by the welcome that awaited us as we opened the front door. I had really missed the children and there they were, excitedly waiting to see their new brother.

It was now early the next evening. I was feeling slightly nervous, as it had been four years since I had last bathed a baby as small as William. I mentioned it to James, who said,

"Don't worry, Mum. I'll give you a hand."

There was a large fireguard in front of the open fire. The three girls were waiting to see their baby brother have his first bath. Mum was sitting in the armchair, close to the fire. James carried the bath of warm water through from the kitchen and stood it on the bath stand. Alan arrived home from work just in time to see William have his first bath in front of all of the family and the warmth of the coal fire. James was standing by my side, ready to give support if needed. There was a fourteen year age gap between my two boys.

CHAPTER 19

A letter to heaven

OVERLEAF: *Nan Farthing.*
ABOVE: *(Top) Vicky at one of the family's many birthday parties,*
a recognisable sight of a cake and fruit flan on the table;
Enjoying some sweets - a time when sweets really were only as
a special treat!

We all had an enjoyable and memorable Christmas and it was now New Year 1977. It was to be a year of happy and sad memories, laughter and tears.

James was realising that his nan was lacking in her usual energy, but it did not stop her getting him his after-school 'snack' of egg, bacon and fried bread. This routine had started when he left Mersea School to go to Stanway Senior School. She would say,

"He's a growing lad and needs building up."

The lovely aroma of bacon, wafting through from her kitchen would indicate to James that his 'snack' was ready. He would still always have room for his dinner with us in the evening.

Baby William was able to enjoy some of Nan's attention, but I wasn't sure how much longer she would be able to nurse him. He was putting on weight fast and would soon be too heavy for her to manage. I don't think the girls were aware how fragile she was getting. James knew she was poorly.

Mum carried on being brave for some time, but eventually her bed was brought downstairs into her sitting room. She did not suffer for long. Her last few days were mostly spent sleeping, and the person she would call for most would be Alan.

On the evening of the 6th of July 1977, she called for Alan to go to her room. He went in to see her, came out again and called me.

"Pix, you'd better go in to her now."

I knew by the look on his face and the tone of his voice that she was not going to be with us much longer. I froze and said,

"I can't go in there, Alan. I'm going to phone John."

I began to shake all over and had difficulty in dialling my young brother's number. Eventually, he answered.

"John, can you please come quickly? It's Mum. Alan's with her, but I think she's dying."

"I'm coming right now."

John only lived round the corner from us, a five minute walk away. As soon as he arrived, I looked at him and said,

"John, I'm so sorry. I can't go in that room. Please can you go in with Alan?"

I ran upstairs to our bedroom, laid on the bed and cried – too frightened to say goodbye to the lady who was really my nan, but who had been a mum to me.

I lost track of the time and then Alan entered the room to say, "She's just gone."

The door to Nanny's room was locked until all the appropriate arrangements had been made. The children were so used to running in to see her; somehow we had to explain that she had gone to Heaven. Although James was ready for the news, he was absolutely devastated.

***

Ada Laura Farthing (Mum, Nan and Great-Nan) was buried on Tuesday, the 12th of July 1977. The full cortege arrived at the house at 10:15am and proceeded to the local church of St Peter & St Paul, where the service was conducted at 10:30am by the Reverend J. Boxley.

The burial took place on Mersea Island at Firs Road Cemetery, where she was laid to rest with her beloved husband, James (Jim) Farthing. There was a large gathering of family and friends at the graveside to say their last farewell. Everyone was invited back to the house, where the inevitable stories of past memories were recalled. It was a time of tears, then laughter,

CHAPTER 20

which was good as Mum loved to have a good laugh.

Arrangements had been made so that the children did not get involved or see any part of their nan's funeral. I even wanted to protect James, who was nearly fifteen years old, from this sad day. Alan also agreed that it was best for James to attend school in the usual way. Their nan had left the house six days ago and the little ones had accepted that she was now in Heaven.

About a week after the funeral, Vicky went into her nan's kitchen, where there was a traditional dresser of that time – sliding glass doors at the top, a drop-down work surface with Formica top, ideal for pastry making, and two sliding doors to the bottom cupboard. It was after opening one of the bottom doors that poor little Vicky found an opened box of Kellogg's Cornflakes. She took the box out of the cupboard and came running back to me, with big tears rolling down her cheeks.

"Mummy, Mummy, Nanny has gone to Heaven and she's forgotten to take her cornflakes!"

Pausing for a moment, I replied by saying the first thing that came into my mind.

"Never mind, dear. Mummy will send a letter to Heaven and tell Nanny I will post them on to her."

"Can I post the letter?" Vicky asked.

"Yes, of course you can."

We sat down at the table and wrote the letter, addressing the envelope to:

Nanny Farthing, 'HEAVEN'.

The letter was then posted in the red postbox outside the Post Office.

* * *

It was difficult for everyone adjusting to life without the person we had all loved dearly and seeing all the things in the home that once belonged to her. I personally became so upset with the memories that I faced every day, as well as helping the children deal with their issues, that we decided to sell the house and start again in fresh surroundings.

Once the house was on the market, we had various people wanting to look at the property and we also started looking at places that were for sale on the island. There was one place in particular that we viewed and I really liked it. The detached house was situated in Mill Road, had a huge garden and enough room all round for us to be comfortable. I nicknamed it The Little House on The Prairie and would have loved to have lived there, but it was not meant to be. As time moved on, we either had a buyer for our place and nowhere suitable to go, or we found somewhere ideal for us, but had no buyer for our house.

* * *

During this unsettled period, there were two memorable and laughable occasions when potential buyers visited our house. On one occasion, the estate agent telephoned and said,

"Mrs Weaver, I have a Mr and Mrs Roberts in the office and they would like to view the property right away if that's alright with you."

"Yes, that's fine – just give me fifteen minutes."
I didn't want to turn anyone away, but after hanging up the telephone and looking into the sitting room, I was horrified to see William had used the ashes from the open fireplace to fill up his little dumper trucks, lorries and diggers. There was a terrible mess all over the floor!

I ran to the kitchen, where there were dirty dishes, pots and pans with only ten minutes before the viewing. There was only one option: it had to be the electric oven! I packed as much as I could into the oven, but there was still more to go. I frantically looked around and saw the washing machine was empty, so that's where the remaining items went! A quick vacuum in the sitting room and all seemed ready, just as we heard the knock on the front door.

The other memorable viewing involved a couple who had a little girl about the same age as our Vicky. We had shown them the ground floor and started to go upstairs. The lady went first, followed by her husband holding his little girl's hand. Vicky and I were on the same step at the rear, when suddenly the dear little girl turned round and spat at Vicky.

"You are a naughty girl!" said Daddy.

"What has she done now?" asked Mummy, turning round.

"She spat at the little girl."

"Oh darling, it's her way of communicating," replied the well-spoken lady, moving to the top of the stairs.

At this point, I took a look at Vicky and realised by the look on her face and movement of her mouth that she was about to retaliate, which she did with a good mouthful of spit that went all over the child's pretty little top. Vicky had now also communicated and, being a good and sensible mum, I pretended not to notice.

* * *

I am not sure how long our house had been on the market – it must have been at least a year – and during this period of time my sadness at our loss had gradually been healing and the children were feeling much more at ease. They talked about Nan with laughter, not tears.

After we had all got together for a family chat, it was decided to take the house off the market. It was full of memories – far too special to part with. I was happy for us all; we would all feel more settled and secure. The plan to move did not happen. Perhaps it just wasn't meant to be?

CHAPTER 21

Yo boy!

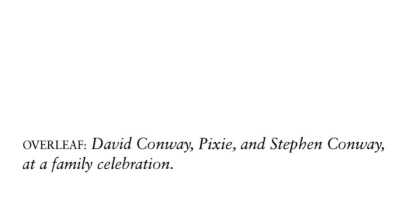

OVERLEAF: *David Conway, Pixie, and Stephen Conway, at a family celebration.*

During the summer of 1978, my brother, Tim Farthing, arrived at our front door with his friend, David Conway. Alan was about to leave when I heard him talking, then he called out,

"Pixie, there's someone to see you. Can you come here, please?"

As I walked through to the hall, I first noticed Tim.

"Hello, Tim."

"Hello, Pix. I've brought my mate David to see you. He'd like to have a chat."

I was puzzled and very surprised. After more than thirty years, I was now facing David – the brother who I was secretly made aware of in my teens, but had never been allowed to meet. Whether that was for the best, we will never know. There was also a younger brother called Stephen.

It is hard to describe how I was feeling as I stood there, but I managed to say,

"Please come in."

I invited them into the lounge, where we all sat down. What a strange meeting! Alan came into the room after we had all settled and he got the conversation started by simply saying,

"Yo, boy!" – a proper Mersea greeting.

David's reply was,

"Yo, mate."

He then went on to explain the reason for his visit. It was to let me know that I would be receiving a letter from his family solicitor within the next week, notifying me that I was to receive some money following the death of Granny Smith.

It was money that Dorothy 'Bubbles' Conway, née Smith, my birth mother, would have received if she had outlived her mother. However, Bubbles sadly died at a young age and her share was to be divided between her children.

It was during a visit to the solicitor's office when the solicitor explained that the money was to be shared equally between Dorothy's two children, David and Stephen Conway, that David recalled the time when he was a young lad and his mother had told him that she had an older daughter. It was a strange story and a lot for him to take in, but her words had always remained in his mind,

"Never forget that you have a sister."

As he stood there in the office, he knew he must speak up, saying,

"There are three of us. We've got an older sister, who was brought up by her father's parents, Jim and Ada Farthing."

The solicitor was surprised at the information he had just been given and now needed to adjust the paperwork accordingly. The following week, I received the letter from Jackson and Powis Solicitors. It was dated the 5th of July 1978 and enclosed was a cheque for £972.29. Today, this would be worth approximately £5,000. I was happy to be able to recognise my two brothers at last, but it felt rather strange when I paid the money into my bank account. I felt slightly uneasy – was it really right for me to have it?

CHAPTER 21

Sophie's struggles

East Anglian Daily Times — Thursday June 14, 1980

Parents accuse Essex head of cold shoulder treatment

No place for you, school tells disabled Sophie, 11

By CHRISTINE EVANS

A BRIGHT Essex schoolgirl, who passed the 11-Plus "with flying colours," has been barred from attending a select Colchester girls' school — because she is disabled.

Little Sophie Weaver — who has suffered from arthritis for the past five years and who has to spend most of her time in a wheelchair — will not be going to Colchester High School for Girls this September, because the school says it cannot cope with her disability.

So Sophie, 11, of Rosebank Road, West Mersea, will instead join her other friends from West Mersea County Primary School at Colchester comprehensive Thomas Lord Audley School — where the headmaster, Mr. Geoffrey Kerr, has promised "to do all I can to make sure Sophie takes part in every subject."

Sophie was one of only six of her 72 primary schoolfriends to be accepted by a selective school.

Her mother, Ann, spoke from their home yesterday. "Sophie was very disappointed at first, but now that we have been round the Thomas Lord Audley School we are convinced she will be very happy there."

Mrs. Weaver claimed she had been given "the cold shoulder" by high school head Mrs. Jean Goodfellow, who "openly discouraged any ideas we had of sending Sophie to the school."

"She made it quite clear that she was not prepared in any way to make any special arrangements for Sophie at all. We expected that there would be some lessons that Sophie could not take part in but we did not expect the cold shoulder treatment.

"Mr. Kerr could not have been more helpful. My husband and I are delighted that Sophie was made so welcome. We are sure she will receive a high standard of education."

Mrs. Weaver said Mr. Kerr had said that timetable and classroom changes would be made to include Sophie in all lessons — including domestic science and woodwork — and he would do his best to make arrangements for the ten-mile journey from Sophie's home to the school.

Mr. Kerr confirmed yesterday that he had already started looking into how classes could be rearranged for Sophie.

"Sophie is a bright child and I hope she will stay with us to take O and A levels," said Mr. Kerr, who added that Sophie was only the second disabled pupil ever to have attended the school.

High school headmistress Mrs. Goodfellow denied that she had given Sophie the cold shoulder.

"We do not have any special provision at this school for pupils like Sophie and we have never had any severely handicapped children here. If I had the facilities I would be delighted to help the child."

She added that the school was old-fashioned and that there would be "great difficulties" in changing the school timetable for Sophie.

A spokesman for Essex County Council said yesterday county policy was to try to keep handicapped children at normal schools.

Eleven-year-old Sophie Weaver, of Rosebank Road, West Mersea, doing her homework last night.

Sign of thanks at | An artistic

OVERLEAF: *Sophie.*

ABOVE: *A clipping of article kept from the East Anglian Daily Times.*

Over the years, there were various mistakes made with Sophie's medical treatment, including clerical errors which caused much confusion and stress. I felt on one occasion when we attended the Canadian Red Cross Memorial Hospital, Taplow, that we were being bullied by the consultant who had seen Sophie. Surprisingly, Alan said very little as the consultant sat behind her desk with a folder of notes in front of her. She looked up and said that she intended to replace both of Sophie's hips and that she would perform the operation at the hospital.

At this point, I spoke up and said,

"I would really prefer to wait until Sophie is older, as she seems so little to have such a big operation."

At this point, the consultant threw all her paperwork across the desk and said,

"Are you trying to tell me how to do my job?"

I was shocked by her reaction, but replied calmly,

"No, of course I'm not. But I want some time to think about what would be best for our little girl."

I looked at Alan as I moved towards the door. I had nothing else to say. I went back into the waiting room, which was luckily empty, and it gave me some thinking time. It had been a long day with some emotional moments. We had a lot to think and talk about, but right now I just wanted to get in the car and go home.

After our experience with the consultant at the hospital, we decided to visit our local doctor. The most important part of our chat was when he said,

"You do realise that hip replacements for someone as little

as Sophie would have to be replaced many times during the course of her growth, which means she would spend most of her young years in a wheelchair anyway?"

We decided against hip replacements – at least while Sophie was still growing, and then she would be old enough to make her own decisions if necessary.

* * *

Although Sophie had been forced to have a year off school during her illness, with the help of some private home tuition from Mrs Jenny Pyle – an excellent teacher – she still managed to return to West Mersea School and win a first prize in class, which was presented by Mrs Judy Buck, wife of Colchester Member of Parliament, Mr Anthony Buck.

There followed a good period of time when Sophie was able to attend regularly at school with the help of her wonderful young friends, Penny Keene, Sarah Lunnon, Suzanne Webb and Pippit Temple-Cox. These girls made it possible for Sophie to enjoy a normal school education, despite her now needing to be in a wheelchair. It gave me peace of mind when I left her at school, knowing that she had very supportive friends.

Hard work enabled Sophie to achieve high marks when she took the Eleven Plus exam and she was consequently offered a place at the prestigious Girls' High School in Colchester. The whole family were excited and pleased about her great achievement. However, it did not take long for the real world to start spoiling the dream – which is all it was in the end.

The day arrived for the interview at the school. Dorothy Farthing (Auntie Dot) agreed to come with us. We were welcomed into the room where the interview took place. It began with the headteacher introducing herself in the usual amiable way that one would expect. The conversation was gradually directed in a subtle manner to the wheelchair and it began to become evident that there could be difficulties.

CHAPTER 22

"I would like you to see our school," said the headteacher as she led the way to the main door, where the students appeared to be changing classes. I was then asked,

"Would your daughter be able to get through these doors?"

"No. I am afraid that she would need some help," I replied.

"I'm sorry. I couldn't expect the pupils to take on a responsibility that may make them late for lessons."

I cannot describe my emotions. During the whole meeting it had become obvious that the Girls' High School were not happy to cope with Sophie and her wheelchair. I was so upset with the outcome and the disappointment that Sophie must have been feeling.

Suddenly, Auntie Dot spoke up.

"I personally don't want to see Sophie attend a school that has no compassion or thought for others."

At this point, we left Colchester High School for Girls with all of us deciding that Sophie would probably be better off at Thomas Lord Audley, the secondary school where the other West Mersea School pupils would be going.

Mr Kerr, the headteacher of Thomas Lord Audley School was very helpful, looking into the ways classes could be changed or managed in order to include Sophie in all lessons. Ramps would be installed where possible and he would make arrangements for the eight-mile journey from our home to the school. What a difference in the attitude and the all-round help that was now being offered!

* * *

Sophie was enjoying her hydrotherapy, which had been recommended by the rheumatologist. It was at an indoor heated pool in Colchester and we attended the sessions regularly. Her physiotherapist was a kind, helpful and understanding person.

However, during May 1979, I received an unexpected

letter from the consultant rheumatologist saying it would be advisable to stop giving Sophie physiotherapy and hydrotherapy on an indefinite basis, as he was not being given the chance to measure any progress. I quote:

"I do not want the therapy to continue unless we are quite certain that it is productive."

We were absolutely devastated by this decision, especially as I had previously telephoned the hospital to explain that I was unable to attend the appointment with him, as my other children were unwell with the mumps. I would have thought that his qualified physiotherapist would have been able to report anything that was not in Sophie's interest. This decision was upsetting for Sophie, as she really enjoyed her time in the pool.

I then received a further letter from the rheumatologist dated the 15th of June 1979, saying he was sorry not to have seen us at the clinic with Sophie, as he had hoped that we might have had the chance to smooth things over, as well as giving him the opportunity to see how Sophie had been now that physiotherapy had stopped. He went on to say that if we felt at any time we could, or would, like to get in touch again, he hoped we would not hesitate too much. He then signed off.

We had been so upset when Sophie was denied the treatment from the National Health Service, which we felt she deserved and needed, that we decided to seek help through a private physiotherapist. We also managed to hire time at an indoor swimming pool, so Sophie would not be missing out on anything that was of benefit to her.

It had not been an easy time. Even the Canadian Red Cross Memorial Hospital, Taplow sent an appointment letter to our address with the wrong name on it. It was addressed to a Mrs Barker, making an appointment for a Sophie Barker. All this resulted in a missed appointment. I got the blame, even though I had telephoned and explained the situation. I was assured that there was not an appointment on that day for Sophie Weaver, so we did not embark on the one-hundred mile journey.

CHAPTER 22

New challenges

OVERLEAF: *Alan's diesel milkfloat and family car parked on Rosebank Road.*

ABOVE: *An advert for Reeman & Dansie from the local paper.*

It was during the late seventies that Alan decided that he needed to get a job that would allow him to be more supportive to us all at home. He usually left home early in the mornings, often not getting back until eight in the evenings. However, he enjoyed his job in Sible Hedingham at H.J Rawlinsons and got on really well with his boss, Peter Rawlinson, so I knew it was a hard decision for him to make. He began job hunting, looking in the local papers, and guess what his choice was? I couldn't believe it when he said,

"Pixie, I'm going to apply for a job as a milkman at The Co-op."

"Why on earth would you want to be a milkman?" was my immediate reply.

"It'll give me so much more time with you and the children."

It was a really kind and thoughtful reply and I probably shouldn't have answered the way I did at the time.

"Well, Alan, if you do get the job, I'll give you a year and you'll be looking for something else, because I don't think it will be challenging or fulfilling enough for your active brain."

However, Alan applied and got the job and he proved me to be so very wrong.

He left home in the early hours every day and was finished by lunchtime. He loved the fact that he was on his own with no worries of a busy office. It was nice chatting with the customers and hearing the sounds of the early morning countryside. However, the work was physically hard with many miles of

NEW CHALLENGES

walking to do, especially on the country roads.

Alan's round was Mersea, Abberton, Langenhoe and surrounding areas – very different to the time when he was a young lad and working at weekends for my uncle (Manny) – Alan G Farthing, Dairyman, Mersea Avenue. During those days, part of the island's round was covered by horse and cart, which was driven by Manny's brother, Fred, who lived next door to the dairy in the adjoining house.

Alan helped Bill Farthing who drove the milk van. Bill was well known for being a prankster and on one occasion, when Fred was delivering milk, the horse and cart stood unattended down Seaview Avenue. Bill started to laugh and said to Alan,

"Go on, boy; lead the horse into the next avenue, just out of Fred's sight."

Bill was the boss, so Alan did as he was told and then returned to the van, which had been parked discreetly out of Fred's sight. It wasn't long before Fred came along and they could hear him talking to himself, saying,

"I spoose it's that bloody boi Bill. I'll sort him out later, you see if I don't!"

* * *

After the clothes shop was sold, it was strange to walk along Church Road and see the changes being made, as well as the new name over the door. I knew it was time for me to move on and perhaps face another work challenge – something that would allow me more time with the children.

Car Boot Sales were becoming very popular and I still had stock that had not been sold with the business, together with toys that were no longer being used and all sorts of oddments that would possibly sell at a 'Car Boot'.

So, I did my first boot sale and it was so successful that I wanted to do more. I now needed extra stock and decided to go to Reeman and Dansie's auction room, which was then

CHAPTER 23

situated on the corner of Head Street, Colchester. It became a weekly event for me. I was hooked on buying not only cheap bargains, but also nice antiques. On the auction days, our house was full of my bargains. Boxes were piled everywhere with items ready to be sorted, checked, cleaned (if they were silver) and then priced ready for selling.

Sophie enjoyed coming to the Sunday boot sales with me. We even went during the winter. She would have a blanket over the wheelchair, as well as a hot water bottle if the weather was really cold.

I also did indoor tabletop sales and the occasional antiques fair. There were times when I sold at the auctions too. Items I had purchased and did not sell at the boot sales or tabletops eventually ended up at Reeman and Dansie's, or Stanford's Auctions, East Hill, Colchester.

My knowledge of antiques was improving and I was really enjoying the new challenge that I had taken on. Becoming acquainted with some of the dealers was an experience. I was really naïve to begin with, but it didn't take long to have my eyes opened to the occasional rogue. There were a few who would take advantage of an opportunity if it presented itself: for example, getting an anonymous bidder to bid up the price of a lot to make the price higher than predicted.

CHAPTER 23

140

James' first gig

OVERLEAF: *'Cocaine' practice at the Mersea Scout Hut, Melrose Road: (Left to right) Billy Dyer on bass, Alan Ward lead guitar, Peter Valler on drums, James playing rhythm guitar.*
ABOVE: *The Fountain Hotel and Public House.*

James had now given up his piano lessons in favour of the guitar. It was quite a struggle to begin with, but with the help, encouragement and lessons from his uncle, Mick Weaver, a talented and professional musician, he gradually began to show some talent – but not without an unsettling setback.

On this one occasion, James had not done any of his set practice. Mick was so angry that he looked at James and said,

"Look here, mate. I know you haven't practised. You're wasting my time. I'll come back again when you can show me some commitment."

I felt sorry for James, but I knew Mick was right. However, I did offer some encouragement.

"James, I know how much you want to play the guitar and I have seen you progress. Now, you need to make sure you put in plenty of practice ready for your next lesson."

The 'telling off' from Mick was the best thing that could have happened. James did then put in the extra practice and his playing got better and better. It wasn't long before he was able to join other musically-minded teenagers. After a lot of hard work, Billy Dyer, Alan Ward, Peter Valler and, of course, James formed their own band called Cocaine.

The band performed for the first time to an audience in The Fountain Hall, which was part of The Fountain Hotel and Public House, during 1979. It was a fantastic evening, supported by many Mersea locals. The boys in the band had invested in good equipment, so the sound was good. John Pullen Appleby and many of his biker friends were there in support of the band and sat in a circle on the floor, nodding in time to the music. It was the first time Alan and I had witnessed the bikers and found them an added attraction to all the young people dancing in appreciation to the modern music of the day. I was so proud of the band!

The New Fountain Hotel was originally completed in 1914 by a well-known local builder, Horace Martin, at Queen's Corner, East Road, West Mersea, after the old licence was transferred from The Fountain, situated close to The Fox Inn in East Road. The original Fountain is now known as Alpine Cottages.

Mersea Island did not receive electricity until the mid-1930s, but The Fountain Hotel was advertising electricity, so it must have generated its own power. The Fountain Hall offered decades of mixed and enjoyable entertainment, ranging from military dance bands from Colchester Garrison to smaller groups, as well as weddings, parties and receptions. I can well remember attending dances there. On one occasion, Jenny Milgate, with her beautiful auburn hair, kicked off her shoes and danced on top of the piano. Her brother, Johnnie, was also there having a great time dancing.

Sadly, The Fountain was demolished in 1999 to make way for housing. However, for many it still holds those happy memories of the past.

CHAPTER 24

CHAPTER 25

Will goes to big school

FANNY ITCHIT

DICK
RUBBIT

OVERLEAF: *William at 5 year's old. When this photo arrived from the school, it came as a surprise that nobody thought to tidy his hair!*
ABOVE: *Alan and William have their picture taken in a photobooth on Walton Pier; An unappreciated drawing sent home from Will's French teacher.*

William (Will) was now enjoying his time at playschool, which was held at the village church of St Peter & St Paul. It was run by four local ladies: Jean Youngs, Jenny Pyle, Joy Flack and Sue Simmons. When they first started to run the group, they got together to decide on a name that would be suitably fitting and came up with The Sparrows Playgroup. It came about because of the name of the church and the old nursery rhyme:

Two little dicky birds,
Sitting on a wall,
One named Peter,
One named Paul...

It was a lovely playgroup. I felt very confident that the children were being introduced to ways of learning and playing that would prepare the way for 'big school' and I'm sure that the other mums felt the same.

West Mersea School was the choice for most of the children living on the island and William would be starting there after the summer holidays. During the holidays, we went shopping for the Mersea School uniform, but there was no real enthusiasm on William's part, which I felt was slightly strange, but then James was never overly keen on wearing school uniform either.

* * *

WILL GOES TO BIG SCHOOL

Will had a lot of memorable times while attending Mersea School. His first infant teacher was Mrs Mottershaw, and others were Mrs Hucklesby, Mrs Smith, Mrs Coxford, Mrs Gibb, Mrs Leavett, Mr Livingstone and Mrs Tarpey.

One day when he came home from school, he said,

"Guess what happened at school today, Mum?"

"I don't know," I said. "What?"

"Well, Billy Chapman had been off for a few days and Mrs Gibb was calling the register. She asked him why he'd not been in school and he said,

"I had gut-rot, Miss."

"We all laughed," said Will, "and Mrs Gibb shouted, 'Billy Chapman, I won't have you speak like that – get out!'" Laughing myself, I said,

"Oh, no!"

"I know," continued Will, "he had to stand in the corridor!"

"How long was he out there?"

"Until Mrs Gibb had finished the register."

"Well, I've never heard the term 'gut-rot' before," I chuckled.

* * *

With all the children now in school, there were usually plenty of funny stories they would come home with. Mostly, I received them with a laugh. I mean, nothing was ever really that serious, or at least not in the way I saw things. Will and the others knew this, which meant that there could often be occasions where teachers would question their messing around in class with,

"What would your Mum say if I told her this?"

To their merit, but possibly not their better judgement, they'd tell the truth.

"She would laugh," which would, of course, rile the teachers even more!

One particular time, when Will was attending secondary school, he had drawn a picture of a boy and a girl in French

CHAPTER 25

148

lessons and given them both a name, all as instructed. However, the boy was named Dick Rubbit and the girl, Fanny Scratchit. You can guess what Will said when asked what I would think of the names selected. It will also not be a surprise to know that I received a letter from the teacher regarding the incident. Seeing it written down made it even funnier! It was a joy to share a copy of his drawings, which showed good artwork, even if the names were naughty – but it made both me and his Dad laugh a lot.

* * *

Kim and Vicky had already been going to horse riding lessons and we felt it was only fair to give Will the same opportunity, so he attended Wendy Mitchell's Riding School at Keston's Farm Equestrian Centre. His friend, Ben Himsworth, also went riding at the same time. After achieving Stage I Equitation with a 'very good', I decided to buy him a completely new riding outfit.

Two weeks later, on the Saturday morning, I called two or three times to wake him up to get ready to go for his riding lesson. He answered, but did not attempt to get up.

"What's the matter with you, Will? You're really going to be late for riding."

To my utter surprise, his reply was,

"Mum, do I really have to go?"

"No, not if you don't want to, Will."

"Well, I'd rather not go. I really don't like riding."

He had probably been riding for about eighteen months.

"Horse riding is an expensive hobby. Why didn't you say something before?"

"Because I didn't want to hurt your feelings."

I was so aware of the enjoyment that the girls got out of their riding that I wrongly assumed that Will would be the same.

When I told Alan, he just laughed and said,
"I'm not at all surprised, mate."

Will wasn't short of friends: Daniel French, Ben Himsworth, Ben Wass, Ian Youngs, Sam Smith, Tim Santer and Nick Dawson - all Mersea School lads. His weekends were now spent messing around with some of his mates – no more horses!

CHAPTER 25

Borrowed children

OVERLEAF: *(Top) A foster girl bathes her newborn in an aluminium tub; a mid '80s doorstep photo (from left) – Alan, Julie Hopper, Pixie, Sophie, James, Will and dog 'Lucy Beagle'.* ABOVE: *(Top) Ted Woolf's oyster pits on The Hard; Orchard Cottage, Christine and David Gamble's house on Rosebank Road.*

During the 1980s, I was searching through the advertisements in our local newspaper, hoping to find an old chest of drawers – one that wouldn't fall apart after being used for only a short period of time. While I was searching, an advert caught my eye. It stood out as it was in large black printed letters, outlined all round with a black border. It said,

"Can you give this child a home?"

There followed a brief description of a young lad. My maternal instincts began to click in my mind. There was an empty single bed in William's room. Yes, we could offer this poor little chap a home. I telephoned the number in the advert. It was Social Services and they said they would contact me soon. I began to think about what Alan would say. His reaction was,

"Are you mad? You've got enough to do with our five children."

I knew he was probably right, but my reply was,

"One more won't make much difference."

It was a few days before we got a reply from Social Services. They telephoned and thanked me for my enquiry. They asked various questions and explained what would be expected of us as a family. I was also told that both Alan and I would have to attend a course lasting six weeks on how to manage the children that were placed with us. However, we also had to satisfy them that the accommodation we had was suitable. It was acceptable in the 1980s for the fostered child to share a bedroom with our youngest son. Today, the rules have changed and it would not be allowed.

Social Services were pleased with the accommodation we had to offer. We had a five-bedroomed house with two reception rooms and a fair sized kitchen, where we all sat and ate round a large table. All of our children were asked if they minded sharing their home with another person and they were all happy to do so. As we had already approached them on the subject, we knew they were all happy to welcome whoever came to stay. This was not surprising, as there had always been an 'open door' policy for all friends and relations.

It was not long after we completed our course successfully that we were contacted by Social Services and asked to take in this young lad who was living in a residential children's home. He came to us during school holidays and every weekend. We very soon realised that he was a habitual smoker, and although we tried very hard to prevent it from happening, it was a losing battle.

There was the time when he found out that money could be made from collecting 'spat' (small oysters) from the mud at low tide and selling them to the oyster merchants. However, he had a plan where he stole mature oysters from Ted Woolf, one of the oyster merchants, then went to his shed in Coast Road and sold them to him.

"Where did you find these oysters, young man?"

"I found them under the Causeway."

Ted knew they were his oysters, but still paid money for them. Later in the evening, I was contacted by Ted, who incidentally lived next door to us. He had recognised who the lad was. I apologised for his dishonesty and paid back the money.

Alan came home from work and had his dinner, then sat down ready to watch television. I thought this was probably the best time to tell him about the oysters. We both knew that the lad was smoking and in all probability the stealing was linked to getting money for cigarettes. The problem had to be confronted, but we did not get very far. He completely

CHAPTER 26

denied taking the oysters and still said they were found under the Causeway (now called The Hammerhead). I believe if we hadn't come up with the idea of unofficially giving him enough tobacco for some cigarettes, he would have continued to steal money or anything else to support his habit. He was not allowed to smoke in the house and we were not aware of any more stealing.

James was now eighteen years old and playing lead guitar in a band with Billy Dyer on bass, Alan Ward on the drums and Peter P on guitar and vocals. The boys were happy to allow our young person to go to gigs with them and he called himself their 'roadie'. To be able to earn this privilege, he had to behave responsibly. I know this played a big part in helping to keep him trying to be a better person.

It was hard work trying to change his bad habits, as during term time he was living a different life in the children's home. After he had spent a weekend trying to behave at home with the family, we would take him to Colchester, where he was picked up by coach and taken back to his residential school. As he boarded the coach and met his peers, the language was horrendous, along with some very rude hand gestures – he didn't stand a snowball's chance in hell! We had to persevere for a long time to even begin to help him adjust to family life and there were still to be many challenges along the way.

He was the first of many 'borrowed children' - the term I used for the children that came to live with us as part of our family. Sometimes they would only stay with us for a few weeks, other times it would be years. I used the word 'borrowed', because these young people who were fostered still belonged to their parents. We were just helping them over a difficult period until the time was right for them to return home, or they were old enough to move into supported living.

* * *

Christine and David Gamble first moved to Rosebank Road in the late 1970s with their two children, Simon (Golly) and Victoria (Bumble). They moved into the strange-looking wooden bungalow called Orchard Cottage. The large garden was part of an orchard and the wooden dwelling was known to some as The Shack. However, it was very comfortable and cosy inside, with a large open fireplace. Soon, they would be building a large brick bungalow in the grounds.

My girls soon became friendly with Tina, a young girl who was being fostered by the Gambles. From that time onwards, a very close relationship was built between our families, with many secrets, much laughter and sometimes hidden tears.

One day when some chicken eggs went missing from the Gamble's, Kim and Vicky got the blame, which they both strongly denied. They got the name Egg Snatchers from Golly and his mate, Ashley. It was years rather than months later, when the boys owned up, admitting to having had an egg fight.

During the days that Christine and myself first started fostering, despite what people thought, we were not actually paid for it. We were given special dockets for the fostered children's clothes, which could only be used at certain named shops, and a boarding allowance for food and necessities. Many years later, the rules did change and foster carers were paid a fee according to their experience and qualifying grades of achievement. So, in the early days of fostering, we were often hard up financially.

On one occasion, Christine had got her social worker going round for an evening meal and to see her young fostered person. I happened to pop in to say hello and had never seen so many candles and night lights burning for one evening meal – they were everywhere, including in the kitchen. Christine admitted to me quietly that her electricity had been cut off because of non-payment of the bill. It could have easily happened to me, but we were on a pay-as-you-go electricity meter, costing two shillings (ten pence) each time.

CHAPTER 26

Another time, Christine telephoned to say,

"Pixie – guess what's happened? We've had our water turned off!"

I replied,

"Never mind, we've got a key in the shed that Dad used to use in the building trade. I'll get Alan to come up and turn it on again."

The point of access to be able to use the long-handled key was under a metal cover, close to the road, partly on the path.

Not long after Christine's bad luck, I also found myself with no water. Luckily, Alan was home to use the 'turn on' key. We managed to pay the bill within a few days. The men from Anglian Water must have turned up to switch our water back on, but ended up switching it off again instead. Did it matter? Of course not!

After much time and a lot of hard work, David Gamble had now completed building their lovely new bungalow. The old wooden building which they had been living in had now got to be pulled down, according to the rules of the local council. It was such a shame, as the old Orchard Cottage had been standing there since the 1920s.

* * *

Our children all seemed to be growing up fast – too fast – as Christine and I were both made aware of on a particular Sunday morning. I called in to return a book I had borrowed. I was asked into the kitchen. Christine then put her finger to her lips and began to whisper,

"I went into Golly's bedroom to wake him up for breakfast and when I opened the door, I could see this young girl in his bed!"

"Oh my God, what did you do?"

"I closed the door quietly and walked away. What would you have done?"

BORROWED CHILDREN

"I would have done the same as you did."

He was only in his early teens and it could have been absolutely innocent.

***

Christine and David wanted to go out for the evening and needed someone to look after Tina. I was pleased to be able to help out; Christine would do the same for me. It was an accepted rule that foster children were only to be left with other foster carers.

The fostered children and two of my girls, Kim and Vicky, went upstairs to watch television. I went up to see them several times during the evening and they were all getting on well. I knew it would not be long before the Gambles would be home to collect their young girl.

Suddenly, the telephone rang. I quickly ran to answer it, not wanting to disturb William who was fast asleep. It was Christine, ringing from a telephone box, asking me if I knew where the children were. I replied, saying,

"They're all upstairs watching the television."

"No they're not, Pixie. They're all on the Strood, ghost hunting."

"Oh my God! I can't believe it!"

Christine began laughing.

"Don't worry, we've just bundled them all in the car and we'll be home soon."

The Strood holds a story of the ghost of a Roman Centurion, which is said to appear when the moon is full and the tide is high. The story of the Centurion varies, but many have claimed to have seen it. However, the children, who were now home safe and sound, were unable to make that claim.

***

CHAPTER 26

I have one more naughty-but-humorous tale to tell about the young boy who was trying to be good, or should I say 'better'. He had to attend a court case in Clacton and his social worker came to Mersea Island to pick him up. I was asked to support him by attending, although this wasn't related to his stay with us.

We met up with some other lads, who were also appearing in court at the same time. As we had arrived rather early, the social worker said we could go to the café for a drink and cakes, and gave the lads ten pounds to pay. They came back to the table full of laughter and handed the change to the social worker. There was now more money than she had given them in the first place. Apparently, when the lady at the till gave them the correct change, they claimed they had given her a twenty pound note. They must have been very convincing, as she took their word for it. The social worker did the right thing – what else could she do? Returning the money to the lady at the till, she apologised for the boys' 'mistake'.

Eventually, it was time for that particular young person to leave our family. We had been able to show him a way of family life. Whether it was a way he wanted or liked, we will never know, but I did see on occasions a kind and thoughtful young boy, especially towards Sophie. He was happy to push her in the wheelchair without feeling uncomfortable – something some young people found difficult.

We went on to have and to help many young people – well over a hundred over the years. The most we had at any one time was five girls. Well, four and a tiny baby. The baby's mother was only fourteen years old and she was placed with me to assess whether she would be able to manage the baby if she was placed in a Mother and Baby Unit.

Well, this young fourteen-year-old was absolutely brilliant with her little baby. She could bath, feed and manage to do all the chores – a real dedicated little Mum. On occasions, the other three fostered girls would look after the baby to give her a break. I hope she kept up the good work when she left us.

Some of the people we have cared for I have been unable to mention by name for various reasons: one of the reasons being that I have been unable to find their whereabouts to obtain their permission. It would be absolutely impossible to mention everyone – some may only have been with us for a week or a fortnight. Some I am unable to mention for their own safety, or confidentiality may prevent me from doing so. The people I have mentioned by name in this book have given me permission and I am grateful to them for doing so.

CHAPTER 26

The mystery of the ringing bell

OVERLEAF: *Jeffery's store.*
ABOVE: *Mersea School as it stands today, with its original bell tower.*

One sunny Saturday morning, Sophie, Kim, Vicky, Julie Hopper, Adrian Wheeler (Ady), Simon Ironsides (Pie) and Debbie Dawson met up along Coast Road at a place near the Monkey Beach, known and named by the Mersea youngsters as The Grannies' Playground. It was a nice grassy area with comfortable benches, used often by the OAPs – hence the name.

After sharing conversations and laughter, Vicky suddenly came up with an idea to invent a new type of sweet that didn't exist and then challenge Mrs Jeffery at the small general shop in the village as to whether they were on sale. In sheer devilment, everyone agreed with this idea and they all put their share into what Vicky wanted to call Old-fashioned Gong Gong Balls. So, one by one, the youngsters went and relayed what they would like to purchase. With cheeky smiles, they asked,

"Can I have a quarter of Old-fashioned Gong Gong Balls, please?"

Mrs Jeffery, standing behind the counter, was sorry to let the young people down – each one allowed some waiting time before the next one went into the shop. Last of all, Will went in with Sophie and Ady. Sophie asked,

"Can we have a quarter of Old-fashioned Gong Gong Balls, please?"

"Now, you are the fourth person today who has asked for these! They must be very popular. What are they again?" Ady, quick as a flash, described them in great detail.

"They're a marshmallow on biscuit, dipped in chocolate and covered in coconut."

Mrs Jeffery said,

"They sound delicious. I'm going to have to get some in stock."

They left quick sharp and met up with everyone down by The White Hart, all sucking on a quarter of Cola Cubes, the most popular sweets at the time.

Maybe someone should take Old-fashioned Gong Gong Balls seriously and manufacture them. They could be onto a winner.

* * *

I will always remember another amusing tale from the mid-eighties concerning two young local lads getting into mischief. Darkness had fallen and all the shops on Mersea had closed, including the Co-op on Barfield Road. Suddenly, the ringing of the West Mersea School bell was heard.

People in the surrounding houses were mystified – the school was securely locked up with nobody inside. Everywhere was quiet, apart from the intermittent ringing.

Two Mersea Teenagers, Daniel French and David Stoker, had colluded and planned it all. The two furtive figures had climbed up the back of the school building to the small bell tower, attached a fishing line to the bell and slid down the drainpipe. Then, they climbed up onto the roof of the Co-op across the road and pulled the fishing line to operate the ringing of the bell.

Len Harvey, the school caretaker, turned up and took a look around. He was obviously satisfied that all was well and went away. Daniel and David had an advantaged view from the roof of the Co-op and were able to see Len cycle off up Kingsland Road. Giggling to themselves, they decided to pull the fishing line again. Len, hearing the sound of the ringing bell once more, returned again to the school and repeated his search.

The boys decided it was time to make a run in the direction of home, so the mystery of the ringing bell was never solved.

CHAPTER 27

Our very own Mersea menagerie

OVERLEAF: *Charlotte tethers Lucy Beagle whilst Chloe holds Rosie Barker in Sophie's spare wheelchair – a borrowed 'go-kart' for many children who've played on Rosebank Road.*
ABOVE: *(From top): Geoffrey, Madge, Jenny, and Henry 'Shrink'.*

During the time that our children were growing up there were so many memories that provided long-lasting life lessons, which will be passed on to their children. Animals had always been a huge part of the family: cats, dogs, rabbits, guinea pigs, chickens, ducks, fish, budgies and not forgetting horses! There is a tale to tell about all the different breeds at various stages of our lives.

I decided to experiment with showing the children how it was possible to hatch eggs at home without having a hen bird to sit on the eggs. Mr Peter French, who lived across the road from us, owned some beautiful doves. He kindly gave me some of the eggs, which would hopefully hatch. I found a cardboard box with a lid, lined it with cotton wool, placed the eggs inside, put another layer of cotton wool on the top and replaced the lid. The eggs were left in the airing cupboard next to the hot tank. When any of us went upstairs, we turned the eggs over, mimicking the work of the hen bird.

This went on for the duration of fifteen days and then the eggs started to show signs of cracks and chips. Little beaks were chipping away at the shells. Everyone was becoming very excited, including me, waiting for a little head to pop out. Unfortunately, one of the eggs wasn't fertile and had to be discarded. The hard part was to follow – keeping them alive with crushed up worms and liquid in a little pipette. We would not be able to guarantee their survival, but it would be really upsetting to lose them at this stage. After having a conversation with Mr French, he agreed to place them in the nests of the other two hen doves, where they would be adopted and looked after until it was time to leave the nest.

One day, Alan was brewing some homemade wine in a large crock pot, covered at the top with a large piece of muslin and left to brew in the utility room, adjoining the kitchen. Our latest pet, a little ginger kitten named Geoffrey, had entered the kitchen in a scatty, playful mood. He jumped onto the pot of wine, the muslin gave way and in went Geoffrey. Luckily, he was saved by Alan and came out smelling of rosé!

We really loved our animals and probably overindulged them at times. I was bathing our little Jack Russell in the kitchen sink, being helped by Vicky and Kim. The budgie was in its cage on the wide window cill, eating some seed. His tail protruded through the cage and the dog nipped at it, taking out some feathers. When the poor budgie went to get on its perch, it had difficulty balancing. I felt so bad about what had happened. We learnt a big lesson: don't bath the dog in the sink if you have a bird and cage on the window cill!

The children had been asking to have a pet rabbit for some time. Eventually, we agreed, providing they promised to look after it properly. We explained that they would need to learn what sort of foods it would eat and then be prepared to collect it from around the countryside.

Alan got the wood, wire netting, hinges and latches for building a rabbit hutch. Once he got started on the project, he decided to build a semi-detached abode, rather than a single hutch. On completion, we had the space for two rabbits. The first two rabbits, Sooty and Mrs Pluphin, were both does (females) and as they were still quite small, we put them in the same hutch for company. Kim and Vicky seemed to be taking charge. Vicky would sometimes take one rabbit to bed with her, gently caressing its ears until they both fell asleep and I would then put Sooty back in the hutch.

William was very keen to have his own pet rabbit and, as there was still a spare hutch, he was allowed a lovely little grey dwarf which he named Jasper – after Jasper Carrot, a popular comedian of the time. During 1983, the RNLI held a fundraising fete in the field behind the British Legion, Barfield Road. Will entered Jasper into the pet show and was awarded a Highly Commended Certificate.

Sooty actually turned out to be a buck rabbit and had to be housed with Jasper, leaving Mrs Pluphin on her own. A few months passed. Kim and Vicky were aware that the rabbits were now fully grown and decided to put Sooty back in with Mrs Pluphin, despite having been told by their dad that this was not to happen. While nobody else was about, Sooty was removed from his own home and placed next door with Mrs Pluphin. The girls were shocked at how speedily the mating took place, but at least they could put Sooty back in place before anyone got home and knew what was going on.

It would be approximately a month before the baby rabbits would be born. One evening, while feeding Mrs Pluphin, Alan noticed that she had built a nest in the far corner of her hutch. Upon taking a closer look, he saw slight movement under the hay and loose fur plucked from Mrs Pluphin's coat to give extra comfort to the babies. He immediately knew what was in the nest and rightly guessed that Kim and Vicky were responsible.

We were all in the sitting room when Alan came through the door in an angry mood, glaring at Kim and Vicky.

"You little buggers must have put the buck and doe together! There's a newly made nest in the doe's hutch with movement in the nest."

The girls looked at their Dad, then at each other, giggled with glee and ran outside to see the result of their disobedient actions.

Turning a profit

OVERLEAF: *The Stock Exchange on Osborne Street in the '90s.*

I tried my hand at various things over the years to try to turn a profit.

During the time that Alan was involved with Mersea Football Club, he volunteered 'our' services to do the catering at the end-of-season dance. It was a simple menu of cold meat, salad, hard-boiled egg and buttered rolls. It was hard work, but an enjoyable and lovely evening.

After our successful party catering, we did get asked to do other parties, which eventually turned into Christine Gamble and I doing some 'posh dos' and the occasional wedding.
One particular wedding was quite challenging. It was in a large marquee and we were serving three courses. We employed extra staff and had to hire the cutlery and crockery. We felt very proud at the end of the day when everything had gone to plan.

The next wedding was much smaller and was at Peldon Village Hall. I had an embarrassing moment when pouring out someone's hot drink and the lid of the coffee pot dropped into the cup, spilling coffee into the saucer. My quick reaction was to say,

"Oh Wah! I'm terribly sorry. I'll get you another cup."

The lady replied,

"That's quite alright, dear."

I quickly retrieved the lid and filled the cup.

Despite this mishap, we had completed another successful wedding which we were proud of, and there was also a profit for us to share.

I was still dealing with antiques and vintage ware when I was given an option of renting space in The Stock Exchange, a well-known large antique store situated in Osborne Street, Colchester, owned at the time by Jim Mellish. This was an opportunity I could not refuse – I only had to put my stock in the unit. Jim sorted out anything that was sold. Alan had doubts as to whether it would be financially viable, but my argument was, "If I don't try, I'll never know."

I was really excited about this new venture and despite Alan's doubts, I took on the challenge. Although I didn't lose money, I wasn't making much either. Some weeks were good, but sometimes I only just broke even. After having a chat with my friend, Christine about the way my business was going, she came up with the idea that we could share the unit and go halves with the rent. I was happy to have her as a partner and we agreed that we should each have our own stock, as our ideas could vary on what would or would not be saleable. Together, this worked really well.

Next door to The Stock Exchange was Cornucopia, a shop which also sold antiques and high-end second-hand clothes. Jenny Lane, also from Mersea, was the proprietor. When I was talking to her one day, the conversation turned to Cornucopia being part of the Scheregate Hotel. At the back of the shop was a domed brick cellar with a well in the middle. The building was possibly part of an ancient farmhouse, which makes one think that it could have originally been connected to Colchester's famous Abbey nearby.

CHAPTER 29

CHAPTER 30

Tales from the milk round

OVERLEAF: *Two Sugars café – an elevenses pit-stop – as Alan would have seen it from his milk float in the late 80s.*

From the late Seventies, the children helped Alan on his milk round at various times, usually on Saturdays. It started with James, being the eldest at about fourteen years old. After Alan had done the deliveries off the island, he would then drive onto Mersea, and collect James at around 7:30am, ready to deliver on the island.

Alan often arrived home with tales that made us laugh. On one very hot summer's day, he went round to one of the houses in East Road near to The Fox Inn to deliver the milk and collect the weekly money. He knocked as usual on the front door, but got no reply. As he could hear the sound of music playing, he decided to go round to the back door. It was enclosed by a tall, wooden fence and gate. He opened the gate, went up the drive to get to the back door and noticed the lady sunbathing absolutely starkers! He quickly and silently returned to the gate, making sure to close it quietly, hastened to the milk float and quickly drove away.

Another time he came home late for lunch, because one of his elderly female customers opened the door just as he was about to leave the milk on the step and said,

"Oh, Alan, I'm so glad you're here. I've got a problem. I hope you can help me."

"What's your problem? I'll help you if I can."

"I can't pull the lavatory chain. It's dropped off!"

He went to investigate and found it was the old-fashioned dangling chain with a handle on the end. He found some old, wooden steps in the garden shed and was able to hook it back in place. It is surprising the jobs a milkman can do!

Sometimes, Alan would call in at home before returning back to Colchester. He had finished early this particular day, so he came home for coffee and biscuits, had a quick look at the Daily Express, and left. As he was returning back to the depot in his milk float and was going down what we call Strood Hill – the hill just before you actually come to the Strood – he suddenly noticed one of the wheels had come off the milk float and had overtaken him! Luckily, the vehicle did not tip over – perhaps the crates of milk held it in balance, but it's another example of the many weird things that happen at the Strood.

Once Vicky was old enough, she also helped her dad on the milk round. Kim wasn't a regular helper; she spent more time with the horses. Vicky's memories were of parking along Victoria Esplanade near to the Two Sugars Café at about 11:00am where they would have their elevenses. As soon as the milk float arrived, the birds would fly around, coming from all directions, knowing that they would get crusts from the sandwiches. Nanny Weaver would also turn up on her bike to give Vicky and Alan a treat of a pack of Cadbury Chocolate Éclairs. This was a regular Saturday occurrence.

When Will helped his dad, they still had elevenses. Nanny Weaver would arrive to meet them and give Will a comic called Whizzer and Chips, plus a Mars bar. Then, after the Saturday milk round was finished, it was off to Nan's at Grays Close for a full roast dinner, followed by a choice of either banana custard with cream, or apricot tart.

On Thursday evenings, Alan would go and collect the money from people and Will would go and help. Alan used to carry a large leather money satchel, which held all the loose change – silver coins and copper. It was Will's job to help count the money once they got home. Will enjoyed Thursdays, as people would often give their small change as a tip. Talking about tips, the last lot of Christmas tips that Alan received before his retirement from the milk round was well over a

CHAPTER 30

thousand pounds! He was much respected and well liked. He enjoyed being a milkman – something I would never have predicted.

* * *

I would now like to tell my own milk round tale. There was the occasional time when I would ask for a lift into Colchester in the milk float to do some shopping and then I would return home in the car with Alan. It was a lovely, sunny day; I sat in the passenger seat with the window wide open. We were approaching Manwood when Alan said,

"Oh look, Clive is just ahead. I bet I can beat him. My vehicle goes faster than his."

Clive did the other part of the Mersea round.

"Oh, really, how do you know?"

"I'll show you in a minute."

We began to move faster, gradually catching up. Alan began to laugh.

"I told you so."

Clive was now aware what was happening and also put his foot down. Luckily, there wasn't any traffic about. Our hooter began to sound as Alan caught up and pushed vigorously on the button. I began to feel slightly alarmed as the two milk floats ran side by side, both men acting as though they were on a race track. For a few moments, I was both excited and scared – two grown men acting as though they were in their teens.

"Alan, slow down in case something comes the other way!" He replied,

"There's nothing coming the other way, I can see clearly. I'm not that bloody stupid!"

As he spoke, he began to overtake Clive. Alan gave a victory V sign out of the window, as did Clive, and we pulled back in. We were the winners of the day: the fastest milk float in the west!

An underground den and a mysterious tunnel

OVERLEAF: *The Monkey Beach illustated by James Weaver.*
ABOVE: *(Top) Simon 'Sniff' Santer; Building works on Victoria Esplanade by Two Sugars café.*

When I look back in time, most young people living on Mersea Island were imaginative and resourceful, making their own entertainment.

On one particular sunny day during the summer holidays, Simon Santer (Sniff) and three of his mates, Stephen Whiting (Fish), Johnny French and Justin Rawlinson were gathered together wondering what to do with their time. Sniff suddenly came up with the idea of constructing an underground den on the beach. They all agreed this was a brilliant idea and the project went ahead, taking them just a day or two to complete.

The four boys chose the Monkey Beach on Coast Road for their location, as it was tucked away from inquisitive or prying adults. They worked really hard digging out a large hole and lining it with wood which had been retrieved from Johnny's Dad's garden – left over from house repairs and alterations. The size of the den on completion was fourteen feet long by five feet wide and it was discreetly covered with sand. This hideaway was known only to their very close friends. Inside, it was lit by candles and I am told it had a cosy look. The boys must have been very good mining engineers because it actually worked!

The really big secret was that they used to smoke the odd cigarette and they seemed to get away with saying that they were sixteen years old. One day, Sniff decided to roll 'home madies' cigarettes and went to buy some tobacco at The Paper Shop. On arriving, the shopkeeper said,

"Can I help you?"

AN UNDERGROUND DEN AND A MYSTERIOUS TUNNEL

Sniff replied,

"I'd like some blue fag papers and Golden Vagina, please."

There was a roar of laughter all round – poor Sniff, of course, meant Golden Virginia tobacco!

Although too young to legally smoke at fourteen, they either turned a blind eye in those days or the teenagers possibly looked or acted older than their actual age.

* * *

The underground den reminded me of a really interesting conversation I had some years ago with Ron Pamment (a proper Mersea Man) regarding his working days as a bricklayer, the houses he had built on the island, and when he worked at Clifford Whites in Barfield Road. It is so strange how conversations come around, but Ron got talking about something which really held my interest.

At the end of World War Two, he was given the job of bricking up an underground tunnel. It apparently led underneath Victoria Esplanade which had been laid before the war in 1938/9 and was known to the locals as The Concrete Road. Ron declared that one day the road could give way as it wasn't a particularly robust job. The tunnel led to an ammunitions room and another room containing a bunk bed and some rare sort of stove. Everything had been left exactly as it was.

This chat with Ron was so interesting that I have never forgotten the tale. I have mentioned it to various people at different times, but no one could recognise it as being true, or even take any of it seriously – would Victoria Esplanade sink one day? Curiosity about this piece of history was really challenging my brain.

After various conversations with many Mersea people about the mystery tunnel, I heard from Mark Dixon that Jim Pullen Appleby (a born local) had indeed been in the underground tunnel in his late teenage years. The actual access had been gained from inside the Two Sugars Café, which had previously been converted from a gun emplacement from the war years. For some reason, part of the wall in the café had been temporarily removed which revealed the big historical mystery that lay behind it. Jim was there at the time and saw everything that had been described by Ron Pamment.

Kim's words

by victoria weaver

OVERLEAF: *An illustration of two horses that Vicky proudly drew when she was about 12 years old still takes pride of place on Pixie's stairway 'wall of fame'.*

How the island has changed over the years: sometimes for the best, sometimes perhaps not. I have witnessed many of these changes during the time that our family and other children on Mersea have grown up. I am not criticising things as being either right or wrong; it's just the way it was.

The children would go off out to meet their friends – on a fine day they would get together to create their own amusement. On occasions, parents would be told what had been happening. Other times, we never knew.

One day, I was to find out that our daughter, Kim, had rode off on her bike with her friends, the Watson twins, Sally and Alison. They had been in a field down Cross Lane, behind the dilapidated, old barn. There were horses grazing there and they had decided to ride the horses bareback without the knowledge of the owner. This was before Kim had her own horse. When I pointed out the dangers of their actions, and how wrong it was to take advantage of someone else's property, one of the girls admitted in a jovial mood,

"Oh, don't worry, we've done it before. It's really okay and good fun."

Had the girls been really bad? That's debatable. Were the horses alright? Did they come to any harm? No.

* * *

In the early part of the 1980s, Mersea Island's roads were still considered a safe place to ride horses, as there wasn't too much traffic about. Car drivers were aware of the fact that they could meet horses and riders and drove carefully.

Kim and Vicky had both learnt their riding skills by attending Wendy Mitchells' Riding School at Keston's Farm, Wigborough, every Saturday morning – until they were able to persuade 'dear old Mum' to let them have their own pony.

The following unaltered and unedited story, written by Kim when she was about eleven years old, tells how the girls became the owners of a horse named Mo.

CHAPTER 1

It was a Friday Afternoon and I was reading the paper. I looked under Horse + rider. Most of the ponies in there were about £500 - £800 pounds but right at the bottom there was one for £300 pounds It said "For Sale 2.2 hh Exmoor gelding capable rider needed phone WM 383206 Vicki said lets ring up, but mum said" you are not allowed a pony we haven't got anywhere to keep one. So we waited til mum had gone out, then we could ring up. Vicki lookd at the phone book under Keating, because she thought it might be her friend tracie. And it was, anyway we rang up, and she said that he was alright and the was nothing wrong but he did't like traffic, he was meant to back up every time a motorbike came past.

Tracie said were we interested in him, we said not really because we have nowhere to keep him.

The next morning Vicki went to help my dad to do his milk round. He delivers to Tracies house. Her mum came out and sked us if we would like to ride Mo until she could sell him

The next morning we went round to see if we could ride him, but nobody was in only her nan, and she got Tracies mum to ring us back

That evening tracie and her mum came to our house. Tracie came on her new pony called Starl.

My mum and dad came outside tracies mum said we could not ride Mo until my mum new he was not insured.

I was hopeing my mum would say yes because I had allways wanted to look after a pony. Anyway she said that if we were carefull there shouldn't be anything go wrong.

Saturday morning we went up to see Mo for the first time. He was gorges, he had a dark bay shiney coat with a cream colour muzzle and his eyes, and light brown markings under his stomach and side of his belly. Tracie got him tacked up ready for a ride. We decided not to take him on the road because we had never ridden him before, we went into The paddock for our first ride. He was good but he kept chucking his head in the air so Mrs Butcher had a look at his bit she said it was probably playing up as it was uncomfortable. So we tried him with an ordinary snaffle He was a bit better but he started to do it again but not so much, he only did it sometimes when he was going over a jump.

Sunday morning we went up to get Mo. We got him tacked up, then waited for my dad, he wanted to come with us because if Mo was nervous he didn't want us to be dragged along the ground if he didn't like the traffic. It was 2 miles from our house to his stables so it was a long walk. Vicki and me took it in turns she walked him home and I walked him back. The first day on the road we took him round East Mersea then when we were used to him we took him on some of the main roads. It was a Saturday so it was rather busy Mo was being good but I could hear a motorbike, I was hopeing it wouldn't come our way, but it did. It wasn't a little scooter effort it was a massive thing. Mo looked round and nearly jumped out of his skin. He suddenly jumped on the grass bank and started backing up into a hedge. The bloke on the bike slowed down down, but Mo took no notice he just kept walking back. I was pretty glad it wasn't a holly or thistle bush. By this time the motorbike had gone, and Mo had quited down. I was glad because that silly bush had nearly poked my eyes out.

KIM'S WORDS

We had been riding Mo for a week now and he was much better on the road so we – thought we'ed go and show my mum. When we got home we all had something to eat. We gave Mo a few carrots as he was so good comeing to our house. My mum came out to see him. She thought he was lovely. Nearly everyday we took Mo to see my mum. We usually leave him in the back garden, but that day we left him in the front because my dad was doing our patio Vicki had gone to get a drink and had let the dogs out. Jenny had gone up to Mo turned round and bit her bum, and Jenny ran off yelping Sukie then thought she would have a game and started to snap at his heals. He didn't do anything at first but soon got fed up of it so he turned round and gave one big kick at Sukie and the poor little dog went flying.

It was quite funny, but my mum didn't think so. My mum told us to take to bed. She thought he was lovely. That night we had to clean the back. While we cleaned it we were begging mum to buy him. I think she was fed up of us because she told us to get up to bed about 3 times

At about 11 o'clock we came down from bed because we heard Mo's name mentioned quite a few times, so I listened quietly at the door. I could hear mum saying "Couldn't we keep him, anyway I think he's quite a lovable little thing And they've always wanted a pony

My dad said "well I don't onestly know wether we can afford to buy him let alone finding somewhere for him to stay.

That night I couldn't sleep I was so excited because my mum was talking my dad into it. Saturday my dear old mum was on the phone all day asking for grazing land she gave up after hours on the phone

When I got home from school on Monday my mum found somewhere in East Mersea. I said it didn't matter because I didn't mind biking.

* * *

CHAPTER 32

Mum thought Mo was a bit nervous and jumpy. She thought it was too expensive for a pony that was like that.

I knew mum was thinking about buying him, but she said he was too expensive.

Monday night, mum went to see Tracey's mum. She asked what would be the lowest price that you would let him go for. I stood at the door ear wagging listening to what they were saying.

My mum said

"I've been thinking about Mo and wondered if you could drop the price a bit Mrs Keating"

"Yes I could do because he's got to go I can't afford to keep two horses at two different stables

That evening my mum had a long talk about wether to get a pony or not.

My mum had got everything worked out and in the end she said we could have him, but it would have to be my sister's and my birthday present.

Mo could be moved in the field on Saturday.

Saturday came and early morning we had to go down to fetch him. He looked so sweet just standing there in his field, but when we tried to catch him he decided he wasn't going. Toni Butcher who owns the stable came and got Mo for us.

As soon as she handed him to us he got wild and charged off around the stable while I was running about trying to catch him Vicki was standing there saying

"Kim try and corner him"

"No you can come and help us. Well don't just stand come on".

By this time he was in the lungeing ring. I thought it would be even easier if he was in there, but it wasn't. There were other horses fields around the ring and the horses came from all directions to see what was going on. When Mo saw them he started to buck and jump in the air, then when I got in there he tried to kick me. I was getting worried because the other horses started to sqeel then Jill who works there came over to help us catch him, we took him some food then he came. The next morning we would have to take Mo to his new home.

It was 9.30am when we go to Mo. He was ready to go at 10.00am we had to back him up because it wasn't that far to go.

CHAPTER 3

It had only taken us 15 minutes to get there. We left Mo to graze in the field for a couple of hours. He seemed to have settled down alright so I thought I would go for a ride. As I went up to catch him he turned away, he did this two or three times and he started to get irritable. My mum was a bit scared so I stayed in the car out of the way. He was really naughty no matter how hard we tried he would not come.

There were a few sticks in the field so I had an idea.

If me and Tracie and Vicki got a stick we could perhaps corner him and then catch him. Tracie and me were running up the field with these sticks we managed to get him to the gate and to stop him running out we put the sticks at the side of us for a moment he stood still and didn't even twitch. As soon as he saw the sticks he turned round and charged round he didn't know where he was going he barged me out of the way and I nearly fell over I quickly got out of the field my mum said I was as white as a sheet.

My mum said "Kim, we'd better go home because it doesn't look like he's going to come to us.

When I got home my mum told my dad and he said that if Mo was not going to be caught and be silly like that he was then we would not be able to have him

The next day Mrs Keating brought the papers round that she had about Mo We realised that when we caught Mo and he ran at us that it wasn't really his fault it was ours. His papers said

CHAPTER 32

that Mo didn't like objects being waved about. So we decided to keep him for a couple of weeks to see if he would behave better.

Three weeks had gone by and Mo was getting better but there was one problem. Mo was in the field on his own and he was getting lonely. Vickis friend Charlotte kept her horse Spider down there but his was in a different field with a racehorse Proby the racehorse kept on biting Spider so we put him in with Mo to keep him company.

Mo was happier now he had company four days later Spider had to be moved out because Spider had hurt his leg so that left Mo on his own again. He soon got used to being on his own.

Soon there will be a show that we can take him to but wether he will be good is a different matter.

* * *

Once Kim and Vicky became the proud owners of Mo, their whole lives changed, as did everyone else's in the family. Owning a pony was a big responsibility and hard work. In good weather, the girls used their bikes to attend the stables where Mo was kept, which was about three miles from our house. In bad weather, I would take them in the car.

After they had got to know Mo a bit better and he was learning to behave, Karen Larner, a school friend of Kim's (they were both at Thomas Lord Audley School) suggested that Kim enter Mo in one of the Horse Shows in the Colchester area. Karen lived in Abberton, about six miles from Mersea Island, and invited Kim to ride Mo from Mersea to Abberton. The idea was to stay over for the night so that they could both ride their horses to the show the next day. Vicky was two years younger than Kim and was still going to the junior school at West Mersea, so we travelled by car the next day with William.

Kim and Vicky tried hard with Mo at the shows, but I can't remember him winning anything – that came later when they owned other horses.

James gets wheels

OVERLEAF: *A maroon Jaguar XJ6.*
ABOVE: *Pages from the Bedford HA range. The cover shows the same model of water board van James drove, complete with amber beacon.*

As soon as James reached the legal age of being allowed to have a motorbike, he couldn't seem to stop talking about it. I knew he would get his way in the end, even though we wanted him to wait until he was old enough to have a car.

It wasn't long before a Yamaha FS1E moped was advertised. As the price was in the affordable Weaver range, an appointment for viewing was made and James became the proud owner of a moped. I was really pleased for him, however, I never got to sleep at night until I heard the '*putt-putt-putt*' of the engine coming down the road and into the driveway.

I think my fears came about because of a terrible accident that had happened many years ago when a young family member had been knocked off his motorbike and died instantly. As a little girl, I could remember the morbid conversations about motorbikes and the dangers. I realised that I must cast this aside and think about how many times I used to get in the sidecar of my Dad's motorbike – no worries then.

James made good use of the moped until it was time to think about a car. He passed his driving test in the early eighties and our good friend, Mike Bracey, had got a Jaguar XJ6 for sale. I couldn't wait to view it. Alan was a bit apprehensive, but James was excited.

When I first saw the car, which was deep maroon in colour, I immediately loved it. The seats were upholstered in real leather and there was a wooden dashboard – oldish, but luxurious. I really wanted James to own this car – and there were no negative comments from Alan. The test drive impressed us all. Mike offered us the car at a fair price, although it was more than what we were expecting to pay for a first car, so James now owned his XJ6 Jaguar.

They were first produced in 1968. James' friend, Jonathan Davis (Hobbit), owned a Jaguar Mark ll. I think they were probably the only two young people who owned Jaguars on Mersea. At the time, the cars were being made popular by Inspector Morse, a detective on the television programme. Hobbit's Mark ll model was actually identical to that owned by Inspector Morse.

James was working as a graphic designer for a firm called Prontaprint on North Hill, Colchester, when he decided to sell his much-loved car. It was costing too much to run. It only did twenty miles to the gallon and any spare parts were very expensive.

His next choice was an ex-Anglian Water Board van with the firm's name painted over with white paint. To the delight of his younger brother, it still had a working amber beacon on its roof, which flashed in time of need. Whenever Will rode in the van, he always wanted James to "flash the yellow light!". The van had many uses, particularly for carrying his music gear when his band was doing a gig.

Scrubbing posts and smugglers

OVERLEAF: *Johnny French (second left) and the gang congregate on The Hard.*
ABOVE: *(Top) Smugglers Way; The Nothe.*

The sun was shining, and the gentle ripple of water promised a good day all round. Johnny and Daniel French had cycled down Firs Chase leaving their bikes at the causeway, ready to meet up with Kevin Mole, Stephen Wass (Wassy), Mark Jones (Jonesie) and Bram Haward, known as The Waterfront Boys.

While they were gossiping away, one of the boys noticed a shopping bag hanging on one of the scrubbing posts. These were used by the locals to scrub their boats. The boats were tied to the posts at high tide and, as the tide went down, the boat was left leaning against the post ready to be scrubbed. The next high tide would see the boat floating and clean, ready to be used.

"What the hell is that bag doing on the post?"

"I don't know, but I'll soon find out," answered Johnny as he moved toward the hanging bag, retrieving the contents – a bottle of Pink Lady wine and a handwritten note that was scrutinised by all the boys together. They all agreed that is was likely to be clues for a treasure hunt and presumed it came from The Yacht Club. The paper, which contained all the written clues, would then take them to the next prize.

Did the young teenagers put the wine and clues back in the bag? Of course not! They had a seventeen-foot dory at hand, owned by the father of one of the group. They now faced a challenge that they could not resist.

The empty bag still hung on the scrubbing post as the boys set off in the dory, ready to solve the clue which would then lead them to where the next prize and clue was to be found.

Every clue took them to a bottle of Pink Lady – six bottles all together. This had been the highlight of their day, a bit of excitement mixed with a reward for the brain power used when solving the puzzles.

They were now ready to return to the shore with their unexpected windfall. Some people might be judgemental about what had taken place on that lovely sunny day. However, these teenagers had used their brains and caused no real harm to anyone, or any thing. They just took advantage of an opportunity that presented itself and was left open to them.

Once back on dry land, they all agreed to head to a place known and named by The Waterfront Boys as Smokers' Corner. This was part of The Old City, past the well-known Smugglers' Way and The Nothe, round the corner and hidden from sight to any prying eyes.

* * *

The part of the island called The Old City still has a cluster of variable-sized cottages scattered around. Originally, it was probably a settlement of fishermen and oystermen wanting to live close to the water. It is even thought that there was a fishing settlement there in the Iron Age. The cottages have now been modernised into very desirable, but quaint-looking homes. At the lower part of The Lane, there is Anchor Cottage (circa 1575), Bluebird Cottage (probably 18th or 19th century) and The Nutshell (circa 17th century). The house situated directly on the left hand corner of The Lane, and mentioned in the 1861 Census, was classed as The Victory Public House and remained a pub until 1906, when the property became a private residence. A new replacement pub was built further along the Coast Road, still called The Victory.

I can remember this now posh area being called Smugglers' Way by the locals. I was told by a real Mersea local that back in the 'olden days' when smuggling was taking place,

particularly on the island, that if the revenue men visited
The Peldon Rose pub, a shining red lamp would be hung up in
an upstairs window. It could then be seen across the river and
served to warn people at The Victory pub that there could soon
be a visit from the revenue men. Equally, The Victory would
do the same favour by putting a lamp in their window to warn
those at The Peldon Rose.

I suspect that Smugglers' Way was appropriately named
because of activity on the water and in the pub, but I still
wonder when it become known by that name and why the
old cottage was also called Smugglers' Way. The adventurous
Waterfront Boys have certainly taken me on an unexpected
historical journey I wasn't expecting to take.

* * *

The old, wooden cottages along The Nothe were at one time
old buildings used as a cooperage, where the cooper would
have made barrels, casks, buckets, tubs and butter churns. It is
thought that the business probably ceased around 1914. I am
guessing that the First World War may have been responsible
for its demise. At the far end of these cottages, stood a much
older building which was called The Nothe.

During the Second World War, a private school was opened
in what used to be the billiard room. The children all sat at
card tables for lessons. Their qualified teachers were the two
Miss Webbs: Hope and Alice. Various parents helped out with
different subjects. Lady Metcalf taught poetry and Mrs Tapp
took tennis, as there was already a tennis court in the large
Nothe garden. Also, croquet was often played. The pupils
varied from five year olds to teenagers. Not an easy task for
the teachers!

Jeremy Jasper was a pupil who attended the Nothe School
and enjoyed the times that he spent there. It was just a short
walk away from where he lived. Although at the time of

writing he is an elderly gentleman, he can remember being taught by Fid Harnack, who was the Art Master and a well-known artist on the island. Jeremy also remembers the teachers already mentioned. Pupils attending the school while he was there were Carol, Jennifer and Mafalda Tapp, Ian Mitchell, Ena Gray, Brenda Hempstead, Rosemary Pelling, Sheila Smith, and Molly, Julie and John Barton.

After an early start with his education at The Nothe, Jeremy attended St Paul's School, London, and then completed his National Service. He went on to study at The Royal Agricultural College. After his studies, in the mid-1950s, he emigrated to New Zealand, where he did very well for himself. By 1957, he was working for the British High Commission in Wellington. He then went into the Diplomatic Service, where he spent the next thirty years in postings around the world – Calcutta, The Bahamas, Canada, Bombay, Jamaica and London. In 1982, he was recognised for his services, receiving The Order of the British Empire (OBE) from Her Majesty, Queen Elizabeth II.

Following his retirement from the Diplomatic Service in 1988, he continued to work until 2009 as a Diplomatic Consultant to two five-star hotels in London. That is quite some impressive achievements from his early education at the Nothe School on Mersea Island.

CHAPTER 34

Deep snow and disappearing whisky

OVERLEAF: 'Skandal' take a short break during band practice in Pixie's middle room. From Left, clockwise: Kenny Gadd, Graham 'Grip' Neville, Bill Dyer, Johnny Morris, Peter Lewis, Johnny Maylem, James 'Jim' Weaver.

During January 1987, Mersea Island was hit by heavy snowfall and very strong winds blowing in from the east. Deep snow from the fields blew across the main roads into deep drifts, making access to and from the island virtually impossible for two whole days. The open fields by Bonners Barn along the Strood caused the snow to be blown into drifts of up to six feet tall and The Glebe Corner was, at times, impassable.

At this time, we were renting a field and stables from Norman and Joan Holmes at Freshfields, East Mersea. The bad weather conditions were a worry. The only way we could get to the horses would be in a 4x4 or similar vehicle. After a couple of phone calls, a generous helper was at last found. Vicky's friend, Sally Watson, drove Vicky to the horses in her boyfriend, Mark Skinner's, truck.

It was quite a hair-raising drive, with deep drifts on the road meaning that Sally was unable to see where the ditches were. At one point, the vehicle went into a very bad skid that made Vicky scream and Sally had to pull the truck over to a standstill. Eventually, they arrived safely at Freshfields, a large, old, timber chalet with a welcoming open, wood fire. The horses were mucked out, fed and watered and the girls prepared themselves for the struggle of the journey home.

Graham Neville (Grip) was also living at Freshfields in a large caravan, which he rented from Norman and Joan. It was parked close to where the horses grazed. When Grip was first looking for a place to live, I suggested that the caravan could be a possibility. The possibility became a reality. Grip was used to living in the countryside, as he was previously a gamekeeper at Gifford's Hall, a 2,500-acre estate owned by Charles Brocklebank in Withermarsh Green, Stoke-by-Nayland.

James had first introduced our family to Grip when he joined the Skandal band as their singer. At the time, one of our rooms at home was used for band practice.

During the spell of bad weather on the island, Grip decided to walk 'down West' and pay us a visit. After crossing a field, he was faced with a high drift of snow. Not realising there was a deep ditch below, he got trapped in five feet of snow. He really thought he was about to lose his life, but sheer panic and strength eventually saved him.

Grip became a regular visitor to our house when he came round for band rehearsals. Band practice night stirred our whole household into full action with music and laughter. Miss Snell, the elderly lady living opposite, said that she loved hearing the sound of the music that travelled across the road. We would often notice Mafalda Tapp, who owned The Firs in Firs Chase, sitting on Miss Snell's low, brick wall listening to the band playing – it was part of her dog-walking routine.

It was not just the band that turned up. On occasions, there was also Gerald 'Fats' Morgan, Paul 'Mini' Cooper and sometimes Fred Borges, who came to listen as friends of the band. The names of the various musicians that practised were James 'Jim' Weaver, Bill Dyer, Johnny Morris, Johnny Maylem – known for playing in the famous Pasadena Roof Orchestra, Graham 'Grip' Neville, Peter Lewis and Steve Timms.

Most of the time, Alan enjoyed band practice evenings. He was really proud when we were able to attend some of their gigs. However, there was one occasion when he wasn't too pleased. He went to the drinks cupboard to get a drink of whisky and found it was nearly all gone. There was usually plenty to drink in the cupboard, including homemade wines. No one drank Alan's whisky, unless they asked or were invited. He was not a drinking man, although whisky was his tipple

CHAPTER 35

and he became quite a connoisseur.

"Pix, some bugger has been drinking my whisky!"

"Well, I have no idea who it could be."

Alan got a pen and marked the whisky level on the bottle, ready to be scrutinised when he poured his next drink. In the end, it became obvious that the boys in the band were 'pulling a fast one', because they found Alan's mark and removed it, had some whisky, and put another mark further down the bottle. Alan twigged what was happening and called them 'a load of buggers'. There was laughter all round.

Cornwall

OVERLEAF: *(Left to right) A view from the clifftop road where
the caravan was parked, you can spot Grip's yellow library van;
The House on the Strand Hotel; Will, Sophie and James on the
beach; James and Margaret; Jenny and Holly.*
ABOVE: *Alan (sporting some '!hobnob' branded surfwear
designed by James) and Pixie.*

During the latter part of the 1980s, James and some of the Skandal band, together with a few other friends, went on a camping holiday to Cornwall, where they stayed in a place called Saint Endellion. During the time of their stay at the campsite, they discovered The House on the Strand Hotel in Trebarwith, where there was a bar and restaurant that dished up excellent curries, as well as other tasty food.

This became their favourite place to socialise and attracted them to keep on returning to Cornwall. Each time they returned with a different collection of their friends, but they always gathered together a variety of musicians and their musical instruments. On one of the eight-hour jaunts from Mersea Island to Trebarwith, if my memory is correct, I think we waved goodbye to James, Billy Dyer, Brefne Jowers, Paul 'Mini' Cooper, Gerald 'Fats' Morgan, Mandy Whiting, Adrian 'Ada' Bixby, Carl 'Boris' Helen and Graham 'Grip' Neville.

The band of various musicians and singers became quite popular at the Port William public house, which was just on the hill, not far from The Strand. The Mersea boys were offered accommodation at the flat in the pub in return for their musical entertainment. This was another opportunity which took the boys back to Cornwall.

One of the memorable journeys was the time James travelled in his Volkswagen Golf behind Grip in his adapted library van, where they would both live for a while. Grip had work at The House on the Strand Hotel and James was going to be working as a graphic designer with the surfing magazine

Wavelength in Newquay. This was a sad time for me and his Dad, as we knew he would be gone until at least the end of the summer season. Sophie, Kim, Vicky and Will would also miss him, as they had never been without their big brother for long periods.

* * *

It was time for James and his friends to leave on another long journey and I said my usual farewell, which was as always –

"Goodbye, safe journey."

Then, there were lots of hugs and kisses before they pulled away from home and drove up Rosebank Road. I said to everyone,

"Don't watch them out of sight – it's bad luck."

It was something that Mum (Nanny) used to say. Alan thought it was laughable, but Mum was rather superstitious.

I turned round quickly and made my way indoors, trying to hold back the tears. Alan put his arm round me and said,

"Don't worry; we'll all go down to see him soon."

Those words cheered me up.

We got the usual phone call to let us know that they had arrived safely at their destination and the journey had been good.

* * *

I received a lovely letter from James, dated the 19th of April 1987. It was nice to hear how well he was getting on with his new job. His designs appeared to be flavour of the month and they were selling well.

During the time that he was living in Trebarwith, James became friendly with Margaret, one of the owners of The House on the Strand Hotel. His friendship with her became serious and he fell in love with her. She already had two beautiful little girls: Jenny and Holly. They both became fond of James and were happy to have him around. Eventually, with things going so well, he moved in with her.

During one of our long telephone conversations, James made me aware of Margaret. He told me that he had now moved out of the library van and was living in the hotel with this lovely lady. My first thought was that I must meet this person that our son was living with.

"James, I would love to meet Margaret, you will have to bring her to Mersea to see us all."

His reply was,

"Okay mum, I'll ask her and see if she would be alright with that."

After the conversation came to an end and I replaced the phone on the hook, I went into the sitting room where Alan was watching the television.

"Alan, that was James on the phone. He sends his love to everyone – but I've got some news for you."

"What sort of news?"

"James has moved out of the library van and is living in The House on the Strand Hotel with someone called Margaret, one of the hotel owners."

"I hope he knows what he's bloody well doing!"

"Of course he does. We must give the boy some credit. Anyway, Alan, I have asked James to bring Margaret to Mersea to meet us all."

"That's a good idea, Pix. It would be nice to meet her."

The next time we heard from James it was to say he was coming home for a few days and bringing Margaret with him. Our whole family were absolutely delighted. James had been missed so much since he had been in Cornwall, although we were always talking on the phone, or getting letters.

It was great having James home again and lovely to meet his girlfriend. Everyone really liked her and I felt she enjoyed her visit to the island. It was horrible watching them leave, but we were probably going to Cornwall soon.

Within a few days, I received a letter from Margaret, thanking us for having her to stay and for making her feel so welcome and at home. She said she would love to bring her two girls next time. We were all invited to Cornwall in November.

* * *

1987 had been a year to remember in terms of the bad weather. After the heavy snowfall and strong winds in January, Mersea Island was hit by a hurricane on the 15th of October, which swept up from the south coast of England and caused severe damage everywhere.

Alan left for work on the milk round at about 4am and witnessed the full horror of the storm. Trees were falling in all directions, making it dangerous for driving. He was lucky to get back onto the island. Many of the tree-lined avenues were impassable because of fallen trees and branches across the roads. As he drove along Victoria Esplanade, he noticed one of the beach huts completely flattened. It was a dangerous time for anyone to be outside, as tiles were being blown from roofs. We lost tiles from our own roof, which caused a heavy draught in the attic and made the entry door bang up and down. Tony Green from Victory Road replaced the tiles and repaired where necessary.

* * *

November soon came around and we set off for Cornwall. I cast my mind back to our very first visit to the county, when we travelled with our newly acquired second-hand caravan on tow. It was not as big as we would have liked, but it was all we could afford at the time. The plan was for Sophie, Vicky and Will to sleep in the caravan, and Alan and I would sleep on a mattress in the back of the estate car. The caravan was so small

CHAPTER 36

that we called it The Pimple.

When we arrived in Trebarwith, there was some sort of strange dinner party going on. There was a long table in the road with people seated all round it. To make enough room for the car and the caravan to pass through, the long table had to be moved.

It was at this stage that James appeared in the road and came to the car, greeting us with his lovely smile and giving his dad instructions where to park. He had become very friendly with the owners of The Port William pub, Bob and Jan, and had got their permission for us to park on their private lane, which was part of the cliff protected by a brick wall. There was a beautiful view of the ocean with Gull Rock in the background.

That night, Sophie, Vicky and Will settled down comfortably to sleep in the caravan while we arranged the double mattress and all our bedding in the back of the Peugeot 504. We felt at ease in the back of the car – it was all very private with nobody around to see us sleeping.

After a good night's rest, we expected to wake up to the quiet of the cliffside with the sound of breaking waves and birdsong. However, it didn't quite happen like that. My moment of waking was met with absolute disbelief. I could see people everywhere, passing close by our car! Alan was also waking up. His first words were,

"Bloody hell, Pixie! Where have they all come from?"

"I don't know, but I need to get dressed in the caravan."

I waited until it was quiet again and rushed to the van to get my clothes on, feeling very embarrassed. The young ones thought it was hilarious. Unfortunately, again, Kim was unable to be with us because she had to work, but she heard our silly story from the others when we returned home.

* * *

CORNWALL

The trip to the hotel in November 1987 was really memorable. Will had heard the tale of The Grey Lady, a ghost that walked along one of the corridors dressed in grey. He was refusing to sleep in the hotel and chose to stay with Grip in the converted library van, which was parked on land across the road owned by the hotel. He spent some enjoyable and fun nights in the comfort of Grip's van, feeling safe without having to worry about the ghost. However, he did enjoy the times spent in the hotel, especially all the good food.

It was so nice to meet Margaret's two little girls and get to know them. Holly was the younger at three years old and Jenny was a few years older. Jenny showed me the beautiful view from one of the bedrooms.

I said,

"It's so beautiful, Jenny!"

She replied with quite a statement for a little five year old,

"Yes, but nothing stays the same."

CHAPTER 37

A full house

OVERLEAF: *Vicky and David with newborn Charlotte.*
ABOVE: *(Top) Charlotte on her first birthday, cake no doubt made by Nanny Weaver; Chloe; David Bleeze in Cornwall.*

Vicky was still at school when she first met David Bleeze. At the time, he was working on Mersea Island for Strutt and Daughters Estate Agents in Church Road. It was situated above the video and sweet shop owned and run by Jim Oliver. Jim had become rich overnight after being a lucky winner on the football pools. He won many thousands of pounds – £162,000.00 was mentioned by the locals.

Back in the day, Jim's shop was part of Howard's Stores, a family-run high-class grocers and wine shop, owned by Repton Dixon. In 1993, it was Allerton Sisters Restaurant and it is now Unique Fish Bar.

David happened to notice Vicky when she passed the office each day to catch the bus to school. As David had recently split up with his girlfriend, the director of the firm, Ray Guest, felt sorry for him and asked Vicky's schoolmate, Adrian Wheeler, for her phone number.

It wasn't long before Vicky received a secret telephone call – well, Vicky kept it secret – and their first meeting took place in Colchester, behind The Castle pub. Vicky and Julie Hopper, one of our young foster girls who had been living with us for a few years, caught the bus into Colchester town centre and made their way to the arranged destination. The two girls stood waiting under the large trees in the car park by the ancient castle and its grand surroundings of Castle Park. The silver Ford Escort XR3 sports car approached up the very narrow street and pulled up beside the girls. David had his friend, John Mills, with him.

The girls got in the car, which took off, wheels spinning, for a tour round the town centre with some humorous conversation going on between the four young people. The journey back to Mersea gave David a better idea as to whether he wanted to spend some more time with Vicky. He decided that he would like to see her again, even though she was only sixteen years old and still at school. She hadn't been altogether truthful about her age. Normally, it would be against her nature to exaggerate the truth, but she really did look and act much older than the other girls her age, so David couldn't be blamed for accepting her word.

David and Vicky went on to have some great times together, including working as extras for The Pet Shop Boys in a couple of their videos, which were filmed along Clacton seafront and in the Princes Theatre. However, he did sometimes get irate when he picked her up to go out, as nine times out of ten she was late. He would stand in the hall next to the grandfather clock referring back every minute saying the time, then,

"Bloody hell, Vicky! It's seven thirty. We're supposed to be there now!"

On this particular occasion, young Will had stopped the pendulum while David's back was turned, buying Vicky five minutes more time. Suddenly, David noticed that he was repeating the same time,

"Bloody hell! Is this clock even working?"
Vicky appeared all dressed and ready to go, not sure if she was late or not.

* * *

During Vicky's last year of school, she came in one evening after our evening dinner, looked at me and said,

"Mum, I want a private word with you."

I became worried, thinking something bad must have happened at school. I was horrified to find out that she could possibly be pregnant. This wasn't a time for anger. How must 'my little girl' be feeling?

"Vicky, I'll have more time to talk to you later."

At the time, all the family were about and we needed a quiet time.

Alan was quite upset when I first told him; he really didn't want to talk about it and went into a silent mood. I tried talking to him again after we went to bed and the reply was,

"I don't want to talk about it."

However, I carried on talking, telling him of my plan to let me attend an appointment with her to see Doctor Marshall as soon as possible. Alan suddenly said,

"Do you think she'll want to keep the baby?"

"I really don't know, Alan, but whatever she decides, we must support her either way."

The appointment was made and I was there with her. Good old Doctor Marshall assured us that everything was well and would be fine for all concerned, including the baby. Vicky was healthy in every way and because she was so young her whole body would be particularly supple and this should lead to an easy birth. The doctor also said there was no reason for her to leave school and that she should carry on with her lessons.

School was no problem. Vicky continued attending, despite comments from other students about her condition. Knowing Vicky, I am sure she gave back as good as she got. Although she didn't attend every day, she was in her last year and battled to finish her exams. The family were so proud of the way she managed to cope with her situation. Kim was supportive – the girls were very close.

David was staying at our house overnight. He was sleeping on the settee, as Alan, with his old-fashioned way of thinking, would not allow him to share Vicky's bed. One evening, Alan and I were on our own in the sitting room watching television when I decided to try and persuade him to let David sleep in Vicky's bedroom.

A FULL HOUSE

"Alan, now that we're on our own, I want to ask
you something."

"Oh, that sounds a bit ominous," said Alan, to which
I replied,

"I would really like you to seriously consider letting David
sleep in Vicky's bedroom. He'll be there to look after her when
she goes into labour – she won't have to call on us in the
middle of the night."

I was surprised at his quick reply. There was no argument,
he just said,

"Oh, alright. You'd better tell him he can sleep upstairs
with Vicky, but to realise what a responsible part he will have
in Vicky's life, and the baby's."

When I told David that he could now go upstairs to bed
with Vicky, he was absolutely delighted. I did reiterate that he
had a big responsibility ahead of him, but he was well aware of
that and I did trust that he would do his best.

Our first granddaughter, Charlotte Bleeze, was born on
the 22nd of August 1988 at the Maternity Hospital, Lexden,
Colchester. Although we had visited her at the hospital, it was
so exciting and emotional waiting for them to arrive home.

Our beautiful granddaughter came home at last. I couldn't
wait to hold her in my arms. Her proud parents both had that
look of love on their faces as they arrived through the door,
the same door that we carried Vicky through two days after
her birth. Charlotte was to start her life of love, learning and
laughter, giving us all lots of pleasure.

* * *

She was just a few weeks old when she was taken on a long
journey to Cornwall to see Uncle James. Vicky and David were
managing really well with their new daughter, but a baby is
hard work, so I offered to take Charlotte to Cornwall with us
to give them a small break. They were both pleased to have

CHAPTER 37

time out, but also wanted to go to Cornwall for a couple of days themselves – they wanted to have a long weekend away.

David was now a milkman with the Co-op Dairy in Colchester – the same as Alan. Being a milkman meant he was finished early enough each day to do other paid jobs, such as car repairs. He needed the extra money now that he had a family and was saving to buy their own home.

We were taking the caravan to Cornwall, towing it with the seven-seater Peugeot, which allowed us to make up a double bed in the back when the seats were folded down – at a push, of course. The night before our long journey was a real challenge, packing all the equipment for baby Charlotte, as well as Sophie's wheelchair and all the suitcases. Again, Kim had to work, so she stayed at home. However, her friend, Becky Holgate, agreed to stay with her for extra company while we were away.

We were now ready to leave Rosebank Road. The sun was just rising in the east and we were all excited. There were lots of hugs and farewells. The car pulled away from the kerb, towing our house on wheels behind us with the baby asleep in the back of the car. We now faced at least an eight-hour journey, but our trips to Cornwall were always worth it.

Our first day began with me realising that I had forgotten to pack the bath for the baby. The day was saved when The House on the Strand Hotel gave us a large plastic ice cream container to use as a makeshift baby bath. It was a tight squeeze, but adequate enough.

Another day, we had a lovely surprise when Vicky and David turned up in his white Ford Granada. What we did not know when they first arrived was that David had only driven the last two miles of the journey. Vicky had driven all the way from Mersea Island to Cornwall, because David had been working on the milk round half the night and was feeling very tired. Vicky was only sixteen and a half years old, not old enough to have a driving licence – although she could probably drive better than some people that had got licences.

When Vicky owned up to what she had done, Alan was really cross, saying,

"Vicky, whatever were you thinking? You know the law. I dread to think what could have happened if you'd been caught!"

Vicky replied, "I was safer than David, he could have fallen asleep."

Alan was getting angry and his answer was,

"Vicky, listen to me, and do as you are told. Don't ever drive on the road again until you have a driving licence."

I think David realised the seriousness of the conversation and he went unusually quiet. The driving episode wasn't mentioned again and we went on to enjoy our holiday in Trebarwith. James enjoyed seeing his family and his baby niece.

＊

Our work fostering teenagers had been put on hold because of the change in circumstances within our own family. We would now be using more space with Vicky, David and Charlotte. Also, on occasions, James would be returning on home visits.

Kim had now become friendly with a very nice young man who was a frequent visitor to our home. His name was Andrew Smith – better known as Smudge. His mother had been a proper Mersea local, which pleased Alan, as we knew his parents. They owned Thorps Cycle Shop. Smudge lived in Colchester with his parents, but had his own car, so there wasn't a problem with him getting to Mersea. He was seeing Kim every day.

One evening, I went upstairs and Kim was lying on the large landing floor with Vicky standing over her, trying to do the zip up on her jeans. It appeared Kim had put on quite a bit of weight and Vicky was pushing her belly down with her bare feet so that they could fasten the zip. Could she be pregnant? I hoped not.

I watched as Kim walked to the gate when Smudge arrived

in the car and the way she was walking made me even more certain that she needed to see the doctor. I waited until she came home in the evening so that I could have a private conversation with her.

She was fairly sure that everything was alright and we both knew that her periods could be irregular, often a few months late. However, a visit to the doctor confirmed that she was at least twenty-two weeks pregnant. No wonder she had a problem doing up her jeans!

I went and sat down for a quiet moment, as I needed time for thought. I knew all would be well in the end, but what about now? Firstly, I must tell Alan. This shouldn't be too hard; we had already helped and enjoyed having Vicky, David and Charlotte. I must have approached and talked to Alan at the right moment, because after I had given him the news, his reply was,

"For Christ's sake, I hope this is the last one. We haven't room for any more."

I couldn't help replying,

"I'm sure we would find room somewhere, Alan."

We allowed Smudge to stay over at weekends and occasionally during the week. Towards the end of the pregnancy, he moved in so that he was at hand when Kim went into labour. To be honest, I loved having everyone living at home. Both David and Smudge were working hard and saving to buy their own houses on Mersea. If and when that happened, I would, of course, miss them all, although Sophie and William would still be at home.

At the beginning of December, Kim had a check-up at Colchester Maternity Home and was diagnosed with toxaemia. It was decided to keep her in until the baby was born – it was due in two weeks time.

Chloe was born on the 19th of December, so she was home in time for Christmas. The arrival of a baby is special at any time but the arrival of Chloe so close to Christmas was an extra special gift.

Willow Cottage

OVERLEAF: *Pat Clarke, Les Clarke and Pixie amongst the renovations at Willow Cottages.*
ABOVE: *(Top) Will, upstairs taking photos of the progress; Before the renovations started; After the renovations.*

The house was full of people, all together with love and amusement. Sunday breakfasts were made extra special by Alan, who cooked a large 'fry-up'. However, to enjoy the privilege of a full menu you had to be fully dressed – no 'jim jams', nighties or dressing gowns. You had to be sat down no later than 10am. Everyone respected the rules; otherwise they had to go without the eggs, bacon, sausages, fried bread, tomatoes and sometimes fried potatoes, or bubble and squeak. It was a proud time to see everyone sitting at the table. Ada Farthing (Mum) had obviously left behind memories of the way we had breakfast in 'The Good Old Days' and Alan was passing on the wonderful tradition.

With James now living in Cornwall, we missed him a lot, especially at Sunday breakfast time. His special hi-fi was still in the middle room and we were able to listen to Fleetwood Mac, Elkie Brooks, Dr Hook and a '60s mix. Will organised the music in the background by leaving both doors open into the hall. James was over three hundred miles away, but hearing the sound of his music playing made me feel like he was at home.

* * *

We had just received some wonderful news. James was going to be a father – Margaret was expecting our third grandchild at the end of the year. They were also considering purchasing a property near Mersea, as a house actually on the island might be too expensive. They would probably rent it out to begin with.

WILLOW COTTAGE

I became really excited, as I knew that a relation and close friend of ours, Patrick (Pat) Clarke, was going to sell one of four old cottages he had inherited and that had been owned by his family for many years. They were called Willow Cottages and were built in the seventeenth century. However, we were to learn that this old building held secrets that would suggest that it was much older. Alan was dubious as to whether it would be the right buy for James, as it had got to be completely renovated, which would be very costly. It was a Grade II listed building, so there would be conditions that would have to be adhered to and it had not been lived in for many years.

As the cost of the property was £25,000, James and Margaret decided they would like to take a look and arranged to make a trip to Essex. I decided to get the key from Pat's, as I was curious to return to memories of the past. When I was a child, I had made visits to see Auntie Lizzie with Mummy – we used to get off the bus after we had been shopping in Colchester, have tea and homemade cake, then catch the next bus home to Mersea.

We now had the key to the old cottage and Alan had the time and was in the mood to go and view. As we drove into the rough driveway, I was both apprehensive and excited, as I wanted this to be right for James.

Well, there was certainly a lot of work to be done, but there was a lot of atmosphere and character. The beams reminded me of The Cross, our fifteenth-century farmhouse in Cross Lane, West Mersea – now demolished. I can just remember living there as a child.

"What do you think, Alan?" I asked as we got to the top of the rather dangerous stairs.

"I don't know what to think. I suppose it's worth considering."

That was a fair reply. At least he would not be putting James off before they had viewed it; he was the one who needed to decide whether it was the right place to invest their money.

After James and Margaret had viewed the cottage, they

liked what they saw. Although there was a lot of work to be done, they decided it would indeed be worth investing in. Work was needed on the original building and an architect's plans for an extension to the rear had already been drawn up and passed, in line with the Grade II listing requirements. So, James and Margaret became the legal owners of 2, Willow Cottages. However, because they were still living over three hundred miles away in Cornwall, Alan offered to keep a watchful eye on everything, doing the various checks and getting prices for the work that was going to be done. I would hover in the background.

There were lots of odd jobs that Alan was either able to do by himself or help with. The fireplace was an interesting project. My brother David Conway was going to rebuild it. At some time previously, it had been made smaller, with a large, old, wooden pillar placed either side. The pillars were removed – well, not exactly – they actually fell down before David had the chance to remove them. However, the original fireplace was revealed, with two large hanging chains, one with a hook on the end, which could probably have taken large meat joints for cooking or smoking. David went ahead and built an attractive round-design fireplace, only to be told by the person inspecting the work that it had to be removed and replaced with a more traditional square-shaped design.

During the dismantling of the round fireplace, some smaller Tudor bricks were revealed. Uncertain as to whether these Tudor bricks should be replaced round the hearth, we decided to try and purchase some replacement bricks from a reclamation yard. Luckily, Alan knew where we could get what we required. When the owner of the yard saw the sample brick, which I had put in an old bag I had found at the cottage, he listened to Alan's explanation about the fireplace. We then listened to his advice.

"Because this is Tudor brick, it could lead to some further research, which could be very time-consuming. The best thing for you to do is to leave them exactly where they are now, under the earth. Just do as you were instructed and restyle the fireplace to square instead of round – stick to the rules and use the bricks that are acceptable. That way, you can't go far wrong."

We thanked the man for his advice and returned to the cottage, where David continued with building the square fireplace.

I phoned James in the evening to update him on all the work in progress and we both agreed that Willow Cottages held a mysterious history – their age was possibly a few hundred years older than was once thought. The Tudor bricks would suggest from 1485 – 1603. Will they ever be revealed from under the earth?

Once most of the work had been completed, including the large modern kitchen extension that had been designed to fit in with the rest of the property, James and Margaret decided that they would live there themselves instead of renting it out.

CHAPTER 38

Birthday Buckaroo!

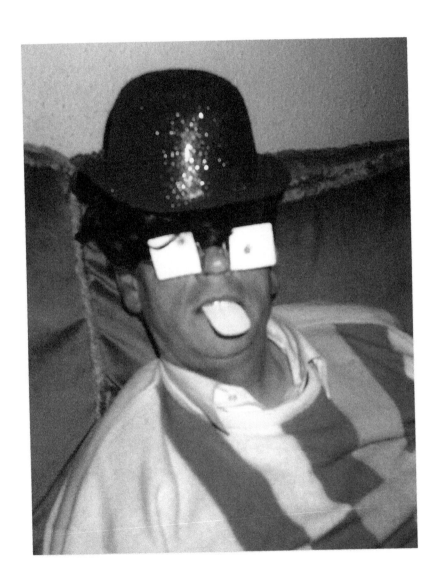

OVERLEAF: *Alan sleeps through a game of 'Birthday Buckaroo!'*.
ABOVE: *(Left to right) Alan, Danny Hempstead, Nick Dawson, Sam Smith, Ian Youngs.*

Will was getting very excited knowing that there were only a few days to go before his thirteenth birthday. We put the Christmas decorations up early in time for his birthday party every year, because the dazzle of the lights on the tree and the glowing Father Christmas that sang added to the birthday atmosphere. Apart from all the family, his guests were Sam Smith, Ian Youngs and Nick Dawson. Unfortunately, Tim Santer couldn't make it that year.

This time, their party entertainment would be the 18-rated film, Robocop, supplied on pirate VHS (all unbeknown to me). After the party buffet and the cutting of the grand birthday cake, they settled down to watch the film. It was during this time that Alan had fallen asleep on the sofa, and as it had become a sport – much like the game Buckaroo – they did as much as they could to him, without waking him up.

On this occasion, he had gone into a deep sleep. They began by sticking ugly eye stickers on his glasses. This was followed by a tongue sticking out of his mouth (giggling away), the obligatory cocktail sausage out of his flies and it was all topped off with a party bowler hat. Finally, the boys took a photograph for posterity. Despite the giggles turning into hysterical laughter, he still didn't wake up, but then poor old Alan had been up at the crack of dawn delivering milk around the island. In the end, everyone's laughter stirred him into action.

"You bloody boys!"

BIRTHDAY BUCKAROO

CHAPTER 40

Together again

OVERLEAF: *Holly holds baby Jack with Jenny in Treven, Cornwall.*
ABOVE: *Jenny and Holly in their Langenhoe School uniforms,*
with Jack; Jack ready for school.

The last journey that we made to Cornwall was for a trip to Treven, where James and his family lived just before they moved back to Essex. Our Happy New Year was made extra happy by the news of the birth of our third grandchild, Jack, on the 31st of December 1990. Everyone was so happy and Alan agreed that we could go and visit as soon as it could be arranged. Luckily, he had holiday time owed to him from work, which meant that we got to see Jack when he was just over a week old.

Alan, Sophie, Will and I were the only ones in the family that were going to be able to make the journey. The rest of the family stayed at home so that the house and animals would be well looked after, giving us less to worry about.

We left Mersea in the early hours of the morning. There was very little traffic on the roads. The weather wasn't too bad until we got halfway into the journey and we began to feel the strength of the wind rocking the car. There was all sorts of debris blowing across the roads. I thought it was rather scary, especially when a large, wooden board nearly hit the front of the car. We were now well over half way there, so it was easier and better for us to continue to our destination, where we would all get to see baby Jack and the rest of the family.

Alan decided to pull into the petrol station, which was just ahead of us. We suddenly noticed that the roof just above the car was being lifted by the heavy winds. The sooner we moved off, the better it would be for our safety.

The frightening sound of the gale-force winds was

overpowered by either Sophie or Will's tapes, which were being played in the car. Bombalurina was Sophie's, with the favourite song being 'Itsy Bitsy Teeny Weeny Yellow Polka Dot Bikini'. Will's album was called Behaviour, by The Pet Shop Boys and it was strange that the song entitled 'Only The Wind' began playing. Alan's comment to this was,

"That's a bloody fine song to listen to when it's blowing a hoolie."

It made us all laugh. There were more miles, and more music – not much further to go. It had been a long, tiring journey, mixed with moments of fear because of the weather, but at last we had arrived.

I will never forget standing at their front door. James had got baby Jack in his arms. He was snuggly tucked inside the colourful patchwork blanket that I had purchased from an old lady, who kept herself busy with her knitting and needlework. We all went indoors in the warm where there were lots of hugs, kisses and cuddles - a lovely gathering of the family.

We had a really nice few days in Treven. Will went to Trebarwith Strand Beach with Alan and James. Sophie and I stayed at home with Margaret, babysitting. The weather was still windy and very cold. Their trip to the beach didn't last too long. Will somehow managed to get his shoes and socks soaking wet and this was probably the reason for their quick return home. The only way we could get Will's shoes dry enough before our journey back to Essex the next day was to put them in the oven to dry – irresponsible, but necessary.

It had been an enjoyable time for us all. Jenny and Holly were such adorable little girls. Both were delighted with their new baby brother. Knowing that they would all be living about four miles from us in just a few months' time was exciting for us all and it made it easier for me to say goodbye. I usually had to fight hard to hold back the tears when leaving. This time I had the inner feeling of relief, knowing it wouldn't be long before I would see them all again.

CHAPTER 40

The weather had improved since the terrible day we arrived, so we were looking forward to having a good journey home – it would probably take us at least eight hours to get back. As we drove off, Sophie's music, Itsy Bitsy Teeny Weeny Yellow Polka Dot Bikini, was playing once again. I was full of happy thoughts for the year ahead.

* * *

On the 31st of July 1991, James and his family arrived at their historical cottage. It was a day that will be remembered by many – those who were still left in Cornwall and the rest of us who were waiting to welcome them into their happy home.

It was all very exciting for Jenny and Holly as they began to explore the cottage and garden. Although the garden was small, it had some old outbuildings and there were plenty of useful play areas in the form of meadow land.

Langenhoe School was just a short walk down the road. Originally built in 1878, it would serve as their school until 1995. It was then replaced by a larger modern building, situated further up the road, surrounded by one of the most stunning views over the Essex fields, plus sports fields and play areas.

Moving from the old Langenhoe School to the new school was very memorable for me and Alan. Being grandparents, we were entitled to follow behind the children. It was an honour to be part of the celebration of their move. Each of the children carried one item from the building. Nick Stanley, the headmaster, carried the school sign.

Before actually leaving the premises, all the pupils linked hands and made a farewell circle right round the school. There was also a memory box being carried, taking all their good memories up the road with them. I was told they also took a large plastic bag containing the good atmosphere. There were only forty pupils in the old Langenhoe School at that time.

However, the numbers kept increasing.

Jack grew up enjoying at least ten years of all the unusual things that went with living at Willow Cottage. One of the memories mentioned by his sisters and cousins, Chloe and Charlotte, was about how they would love digging for treasure in the back garden and surrounding grounds, finding all sorts of bits and pieces: glass bottles, broken vases and old tins.

It's those simple things that children enjoy that never gets old. Even today, with all the technology and devices they have, the grandchildren are often happiest messing around in the earth, as was I when I was their age.

CHAPTER 40

CHAPTER 41

A car on fire and a gun

There came a time in the early 1990s when Alan and I decided to foster again. At first, we were only going to foster teenage girls. However, we did agree to have Richard Nicholson after a very persuasive telephone conversation with his dad, who also lived on Mersea and promised to give us back-up support if necessary. It was all agreed by Social Services, and Richard arrived. Unlike a lot of youngsters who came to stay with us, Richard had good smart clothes and did not appear to be short of anything materially. He seemed to have a way with him where he got on with everyone, although he did push people's boundaries, which annoyed Alan at times.

It did not take long to find out that there were occasions when he was skipping school, usually to work on old cars. Academically, his grades were low, but he was good at most practical work. Alan's car had been playing up and Richard thought he knew what the problem was. I was working in the kitchen when the door flew open and Richard shouted,

"Quick, the car's on fire!"

He grabbed the washing-up bowl, which still contained dirty water and ran out to the car, which had flames leaping out from the open bonnet. I stood watching in horror as he threw the dirty washing-up water onto the car. Luckily, it put the fire out and the damage was minimal, but it was scary.

Another time Richard found himself in trouble was when one of the teenage girls who was living with us approached me and said that Richard had given her some cannabis in exchange for cooking his breakfast. I found this strange, as these two did not get on particularly well – was she trying to get him in trouble? I had a problem and wanted some thinking time to work out how to deal with it. Firstly, I needed to see what he had given her (if he had). She produced some tissue paper, screwed up tightly. It contained something the size of a tiny rabbit poo. I took charge of the tiny twisted parcel and threatened to tell the police. After much thought, I felt the police really would be able to deal with the situation better than us or Social Services.

I telephoned West Mersea Police Station and explained what had happened. They said they would call round and have a word with the two teenagers. Mersea Police were always ready to help, or work with our youngsters. Often, during a cleverly worded conversation, it was surprising how much information the young people would unwittingly divulge. I don't think anything of interest came to light, but Richard and the young girl were told what the consequences could be and that the police would be visiting the house again to make sure they were both behaving.

***

Richard and his good friend Louis, spent most of the summer holidays with Sophie. They took her everywhere, even places where a wheelchair couldn't normally go. They made it happen, taking her through fields, over ditches and to the caravan sites. She was able to go to Bert Stocks' Fair at the West Mersea Regatta, where they made sure she went on all the rides and amusements. It's a good job that I didn't see all that went on, as I would probably have gone mad!

To me, Richard was a special person. I always saw his kind and gentle side, so I was able to forgive some of the mad reckless situations he got into. He had been out all one evening and on his return home came flying through the front door shouting,

CHAPTER 41

"Come and see what I've got!"

I went through to the hall and saw that Richard was holding a terrible-looking gun – something you would probably only see in a wartime movie.

"Where the hell did you get that, Richard?"

He had a broad grin on his face when he answered.

"Oh, I did a swap with this soldier friend of mine."

He had swapped it with a spare part from an old car. I was so horrified with the object he was holding, I shouted to Alan to come into the hall. When he saw the gun, his first reaction was,

"Get that bloody thing out of the house!"

Richard's happy smile faded. I then spoke up.

"Please, let's all calm down, I think we should try and get in touch with Keith."

It was getting late, but luckily Keith (Richard's father) answered the phone. After a short conversation, he asked to talk to Alan. It was decided that the illegal weapon should be stored in our attic overnight and Keith would take it to Mersea Police Station, with Richard, first thing in the morning.

Keith arrived as promised, carrying an old blanket to cover the gun and stand it was attached to. I waved goodbye, breathing a sigh of relief as they left to put things right with the law. I never did hear what happened after the police took charge.

CHAPTER 42

More borrowed children

OVERLEAF: *Alan and Pixie receiving a Long Service Award for their fostering, presented to them by TV presenter Jeremy Spake.*
ABOVE: *Sophie, Diane Brownlie and Dawn Workman hitching their way to Scotland.*

Fostering teenagers was a challenge, but very rewarding. Our own five children played a large part in guiding the young people along the right track. Most of the time, they were able to show a positive attitude with the way they behaved – rarely were they influenced by the new guests.

I have already told a few stories of the 'borrowed children' that had become part of our life, but I realised that a complete chapter was needed to demonstrate how rewarding our life was once we had managed to deal with some very colourful language and occasionally unacceptable rude behaviour.

I have an unusual tale to tell. I am unable to mention any names, but the story is true. It concerns a young person who eventually left us able to behave in an acceptable manner and I am sure she would never repeat what she did on this one particular occasion.

There were three young teenagers staying with us. They went to the village intending to spend their pocket money on a Saturday morning. After about an hour, two of the girls returned home. They arrived in the kitchen, giggling.

I asked, "Where is ____?"

The girls went quiet and one of them answered me, saying,

"Oh, she's in the disabled toilet at the library having a shag with some boy."

I was horrified at what I had just heard.

"They pretended there was someone disabled outside who needed the key and it was handed over to them."

I had never been in this sort of situation before and my

guess was neither had any other foster carer. I would have to deal with it when the young person came back home.

When she returned, I questioned everything that I had been told. At first, it was denied, then silence, which gave me time to point out the dangers and consequences of her actions. My biggest argument was that she was too good to let anyone treat her in this manner and told her never to lower herself to do it again. She replied,

"I'm sorry. I really won't go there again."

* * *

Another story goes back to 1994. Sophie, who was now twenty-five years old, and our two fostered teenagers, Diane Brownlie and Dawn Workman, went on a hitch-hiking ride to boost the Youth Shelter and Enquiry Service funds. It was quite challenging for Diane and Dawn, as they were accompanying Sophie on a twenty-four-hour 'jail break'. The idea for this was to travel as far as possible from Colchester without spending any money. At the time, Sophie was a Drama Student at Colchester Institute and a wheelchair user. The three girls managed to get to Scotland and back by train. They jumped the trains – not an easy task with the wheelchair!

Their first stop was at the police station, where they hoped they could stay for the night. However, the police contacted a Christian-run hostel, where they were accommodated overnight. They returned back to Colchester by train within the stated twenty-four hours, with over £200, which was raised by donations received on the journey. Both Alan and I were so proud of Sophie and our two fostered teenagers and how well they managed with Sophie and her wheelchair.

* * *

CHAPTER 42

Julie Hopper had been part of our family for five years, but not long after she first came to stay, Vicky decided to invent a ghostly tale regarding the bedroom that the girls shared. Their room was a good size and had all the things that most young people desired: television, video player and stereo system.

The story that Vicky told Julie was that their bedroom had at one time belonged to her nan, which was absolutely true. What wasn't the truth was that Vicky claimed that Nan died in the bedroom and, on occasions, returned in the form of a ghost. The family were totally unaware of this fabricated tale until one afternoon when I collected both Kim and Vicky from horse riding. As we drove into Rosebank Road in the car, we saw Julie sitting on the grass verge. As soon as the car stopped, Julie ran to see me as I got out of the driver's seat. She looked close to tears as she said,

"The ghost in the bedroom threw a riding hat at me!"

I was absolutely dumbfounded at the way Julie was behaving and by what she had said. At this point, Vicky spoke up,

"Julie, I was joking! There isn't really a ghost in our bedroom. I wouldn't be able to sleep if I thought it was haunted."

"Why did the riding hat hit me, then?"

Kim started to laugh and pointed out that she had also been hit by the hat one day – because the speaker, which was secured to the wall, was often used as a shelf for their riding hats. The vibration from the loud music would cause the hat to slide off its perch.

* * *

One teenager that deserves a mention was very difficult to manage when she first came to live with us, but after a few years she turned herself around and the whole family felt proud to have been a part of re-educating her to a normal way of living.

Some of her misdemeanours started within a few weeks of her arrival. A box of small plants was placed on the window cill in the bedroom. I immediately realised they were cannabis plants. I asked her,

"What are those plants called on your window cill?"

"Oh, they're pretty daisy-type plants."

"Well, I'm sure I know what the plants are," I replied, "and they are certainly not daisy. If you don't remove them by tomorrow, I'll call in the police."

Before the next day came, the plants had gone.

Another time, Alan was on his way home from work when he passed our same young person on an extremely expensive bicycle. When she arrived home, he asked her to whom the bicycle belonged. Her answer was that her best friend had loaned it to her and she would return it to school the next day. Alan offered to return the bike and give her a lift in the car. The offers were refused, which was puzzling. He began to wonder what was really going on – was she telling the truth?

I decided to contact Colchester Police and found out that a bicycle identical in every way had been reported stolen from an address in Colchester. I questioned our young person about the bike and she said she had returned it to 'her friend'. After I explained that the police were now involved, I was told it had been taken to a second-hand shop and had been sold. When I asked for the money, I was told she had spent it.

My next move was to return to the second-hand shop. If the bike was still there, I would buy it back. Luckily, it was still available. I purchased it and returned it to the Colchester Police, who contacted the owner. She was very grateful to receive her property back. She had at one time been in foster care herself and was willing to forget about the whole incident.

An old family saying comes to mind: "There's a little bit of bad in the best of us and a little bit of good in the worst of us."

This was another young person who came good in the end.

CHAPTER 42

Langenhoe School

OVERLEAF: *Jack and Chloe.*
ABOVE: *(Top) The Art Café as it stands today opposite the church of St Peter & St Paul; Aerial view of Church Road corner before shops and flats development; The empty site as it was on the corner of Church Road.*

By the mid-1990s, Langenhoe School, being known for its good reputation, had attracted our two granddaughters, Charlotte and Chloe. They had gone to West Mersea School and, although there were no complaints academically, both girls at different times had been made to feel uncomfortable by some challenging language and unfair interaction from a couple of Mersea students. This was occurring quite frequently – a type of bullying.

Charlotte and Chloe both enjoyed the time they spent at Langenhoe School and were able to meet up with their cousins, Jack and Holly.

Charlotte had good memories of taking part in a few plays. One was called Yanomamo, which was about the Amazon forest, and another was entitled The Great Fire of London. Another memory was having to stand outside Mr Stanley's office when she had been naughty. She found this embarrassing, especially if other pupils passed by and saw her standing there, as they knew she was in trouble.

Mr Stanley smoked a pipe and when the door was opened, the smell of the tobacco often wafted into the corridor. How times have changed regarding the rules of smoking – totally inappropriate by today's standards! However, there was a feeling of respect and praise towards Mr Stanley and the other teachers.

Charlotte was one of the pupils to be taught in the main school hall as the amount of pupils increased. A mixed group of years five and six operated in the hall, with Mr Stanley teaching a class of about twenty. At lunch time, another part of the hall was used for the dining area, where the tables seated eight people. Pupils from years five and six became known as 'The Servers'. The dinner lady brought the food to the tables and the young servers dished up the food on nice china plates. Everyone had been taught the correct dining etiquette, something to be proud about.

* * *

Jack's memories of his early school days were of the summer fetes and fayres. One year, his mother won the raffle. The prize was a beautiful handmade quilt that was made and donated by one of the teachers, Mrs Wilmott. It has been known over the years in the Weaver family as The Wilmott Quilt and it is still used.

Jack enjoyed the school story tree, which had been carved into a seat with arms. This became a memory for many pupils. Mrs Roberts would take the class outside during the summer months and read a story while sitting on the seat, with the children sitting cross-legged on the grass. During the Millennium Year, a dome type structure was built next to the story tree.

As Christmas approached, Father Christmas stood giving out gifts by the balcony that was situated above the office. A Christmas tree stood on the balcony, decorated with baubles, lights and gold coins. Once some of the youngsters realised the gold coins contained chocolates, they disappeared into tummies.

There was a kiln in the hallway alcove, where Jack remembers making some creative pottery. It is highly likely that his mum has kept his finished items.

* * *

CHAPTER 43

Chloe has many memories of the school too. She also experienced the embarrassment of having to wait outside Mr Stanley's office for being a naughty girl. She was caught kissing a boy at lunchtime by one of the dinner ladies. Both Chloe and the young lad had to spend time in the corridor before they were told off by the Headmaster. It was a situation that neither of them wanted to face again.

Chloe also tried to learn to play the flute, but her teacher had a strong Scottish accent that Chloe was unable to fully understand. Sadly, she was too shy to tell her teacher, which meant that she never did get to actually play the flute properly. Eventually, Chloe, Charlotte and Jack all ended up playing recorders: treble and tenor. Mrs Woodhurst was their teacher.

There was the time Chloe caught her foot in a rabbit hole on the school field. Unfortunately, she fell over, twisting her ankle at the same time. She was rescued with the use of a chair borrowed from the office, which luckily had wheels on the legs. There was some laughter as she was pushed along back to the office, where her mum collected her in the car and took her to the hospital for a check up. The diagnosis was torn ligaments.

The last memory for Chloe was dressing up to look like Mr Stanley, with the rest of the class, as a tribute to him on his retirement from the school. It was a lovely gesture that made him laugh a lot. The boys and girls were wearing moustaches and glasses, as well as clothes that were a close match to his. It was a real fun farewell that will never be forgotten.

* * *

Charlotte had approximately one year left at Langenhoe when her little sister, Georgina (George), first started at the school. George was five years younger than Charlotte and stayed at Langenhoe School until she moved on to senior school.

George's memories of Langenhoe School were mostly with the new headteacher, Mrs Vine. She enjoyed her first year with

Mrs Roberts and also created many enjoyable memories during the rest of her time there. George always looked forward to purchasing tray-baked mixed-flavoured cakes from cook, Mrs O'Shea, which could be bought in the foyer at break times.

She remembers the summer fete one year, when they had a 'wonky bike' where people could have a fun ride. If you turned the handlebar to the right, it went left, and vice versa. Quite a challenge!

She also decided to enter a painting and drawing competition that had been organised by Tesco. Her Mum, Vicky, brought home the entry form. George did a drawing of West Mersea beach and submitted her picture with the form. The prize that could be won was a computer for the school. Two weeks later, everyone was delighted to hear that George had won. We were all so proud and pleased that the school would benefit.

A pleasurable outdoor learning facility was the school pond. The children could watch the birds and collect pond water in trays so that further studies could be made back in the classroom. A lesson that was enjoyed by the whole class was seeing the frog spawn develop into tadpoles.

A memorable character for everyone was Mrs Leek, the receptionist, a lovely lady who had crazy haircuts with bright, spiky coloured hair – sometimes pink, orange, red or blue!

* * *

During the end of the '90s, with Christmas fast approaching, Mr Stanley and his staff at Langenhoe School had been unable to arrange a date with the school cook to do the traditional evening Christmas dinner. Margaret (Maggie) Weaver, being a professional chef, said she would be pleased to help out.

It was a night to remember. They turned the classroom into 'Langenhoe Brasserie', putting lots of tables together and setting it up as a restaurant. A week prior to the actual dinner,

CHAPTER 43

everyone was given a printed menu with three starters, three mains and three puddings to choose from. Maggie did most of the preparations at home, but finished the cooking in the school kitchen. John and Mel Sawdon, and Alan Frost from Abberton Car Sales organised the wine, and a parent whose business was flashy cars picked everyone up in a limo. During the evening, James entertained between courses playing his mandolin and guitar – it was a grand, memorable evening.

* * *

After the Christmas holiday and into another year, our son Will and his girlfriend, Kate Whiteman, were both doing a degree in Art and Design at Colchester Institute. They chose to spend four sessions at Langenhoe School over a month, looking into how art and design is taught at Key Stage Two. It was really helpful to their studies.

Will recalls that during their study time there, Jenny had her bicycle stolen from the back garden at Willow Cottage. Being right on the main road and having a large entrance driveway to one side, it was easy for anyone who was that way inclined to take advantage and walk away with a free bike. However, a strange bit of luck turned up two weeks later, when James and Maggie were driving along the road five miles from their home. James suddenly said,

"Look, there's Jenny's bike!"

There was no mistaking the bike. It had small wheels and was bright blue in colour. James stopped the car and challenged the youngsters, who totally denied any knowledge of it being taken. James then said,

"Alright, I'll phone the police and we'll have a chat."

At this point the bike was dropped and they all ran off. James retrieved it, put it in the back of the car and drove home. A lucky day!

* * *

In 2003, James and Maggie became the owners of No 2
Coast Road. The property had previously been a shoe shop,
then Briggs Art and Bookshop. Today it is The Art Café.
With James' background in art and Maggie's talent and
qualifications as a chef, it wasn't too surprising that The Art
Café became a really successful business. When they took it
over, a lot of work was needed to refurbish it. After many
hours of labour, internally and externally, they finally made it
into the café everyone is familiar with.

The shop development with flats above was originally
completed in 1971. It was much more modern than the buildings
surrounding it. However, we do have to move with the times.
As my granddaughter Jenny, chef and director at The Art Café,
said when she was young, "Nothing stays the same."

Customers sitting in the sunshine on the forecourt of the
café (overlooking the thousand-year-old church, with the
beautiful, old trees overhanging the road) probably wouldn't
know that the place where they are enjoying good food was
once part of agricultural ground used for a seed-growing
business. The fields stretched over ten acres of land, extending
into St Peter's Road, and backing onto the beautiful Yew Tree
House, which was built in early Victorian times, just on the
Coast Road bend.

In times past, Yew Tree House got most of their household
water from the rain that fell onto the house roof into the
gutters, ending up in water butts ready for domestic use.
However, their drinking water would be collected from
St Peter's Well, situated across the road by what today is called
the Monkey Beach. St Peter's Well is still there to be seen.

* * *

CHAPTER 43

I have just been on a quick historical journey in this short chapter, but Mersea is full of various tales, some of which I have mentioned in past pages. While writing, what I can say is that I would not want to go back to some of the historical ways of living. Our family, the Farthings, have been on the island for well over two hundred years. My grandfather, Jim, was a poultry farmer and seed grower. I am sure that if he was here today, our modern style of living would give preference over well water, horse and carts, outside toilets with 'bucket and chuck it,' oil lamps, coal fires and so on. There is a lot in the world to be thankful for today.

CHAPTER 44

Horses, *a helicopter and hospital*

OVERLEAF: *Pixie leading 'Ben' with Ludovic..*
ABOVE: *(Top) Vicky and Charlotte with 'Fletcher'; Vicky, Kim and Chloe in a cart led by 'Horace'.*

From the time that Kim and Vicky owned their first pony, Mo, until this very day, they have always owned horses.

Their busiest time began in the mid-nineties, when they decided to open their own riding stables, which in those days was part of Coopers Beach Caravan Park. Over the years, the girls had competed and won various certificates issued by The British Horse Society, which entitled them to hold a licence to keep a riding establishment – the premises known as Hall Farm, Church Lane, East Mersea.

When they first started their business, there were enough stables for the amount of horses being used, but their popularity began to grow, so their dad turned a large unused barn into another four stables. Gradually, the number of horses and ponies numbered at least a dozen – an awful lot of hard work. However, they did have the support of Alan, as well as David and Smudge. Charlotte and Chloe were now both old enough to ride the small ponies.

There was always a lot of excitement at the arrival of a new horse, or pony. At the Cattle Market in Wyncolls Lane, Colchester, the girls made a totally unplanned, spur-of-the-moment bid for a gorgeous little 11.2 hand Strawberry Roan. Just because they felt sorry for him, they bid up to £225. The hammer came down and he was theirs! They had no transport to get him home, but they were able to arrange transport with a very nice man who agreed to get him back to Coopers Beach.

David was the first person to attempt to mount Charlie and he got bucked off fairly quickly. After mounting for the third time, the pony quietened down. A local onlooker said,

"Christ, mate he's buckarooed loike a gooden!"

He was used each day by Kim and Vicky for a week or so, but then they took him to Eileen Smith at the riding centre in Boxted to be schooled.

The horse that I personally got involved with was Ben, a lovely 15.2 hand Piebald Cob, because the girls were not in a position at the time to invest any more money. He was really more than I could afford, but after seeing him I couldn't stop thinking about how useful he would be. He was used to driving a cart, as well as being a nice ride.

* * *

Felix Tsang became friendly with Sophie at Essex University when they were both doing a Postgraduate Diploma in Computing. Felix came from Hong Kong and was looking for accommodation. He wasn't having too much luck, so we offered him the use of our caravan which he was pleased to accept.

When Felix heard about Ben, the Piebald Cob we had been to see at Great Dunmow, he said he would really like to go and see him. Apparently, Felix's father was very interested in horses and racing. If Felix liked the look of the horse, he said he would be prepared to go halves with me on the price, which was £1500.00, or £750 each. We could both become the owners with no real overhead expenses, as we would be letting the girls have him on loan.

Alan drove us over to Great Dunmow to view the horse, while it grazed in the field. As Kim and Vicky had already ridden him, we made a decision with Felix to purchase him and agreed to collect him in the horsebox at the weekend. Felix could not wait to get in touch with his father in Hong Kong to tell him that he was now a part owner of a horse called Ben.

After acquiring Ben, the girls went on to purchase a really useful old cart from Mrs Sunnocks, who owned

CHAPTER 44

East Mersea Hall, adjoining the stables. The large cart had seating fitted all round, which allowed them to use it to give rides to people. East Mersea Hall was a beautiful fifteenth century Elizabethan Manor House, with many surrounding acres of land. I always enjoyed the beautiful garden and nearby woodlands of this age-old countryside and lovely church, which has parts dating back to the twelfth century.

* * *

It was during the summer of 1996 that we agreed to support two French teenagers from a school in France that catered for teenagers with social and behavioural difficulties. Ludovic arrived in England on Monday, the 3rd of June and we met him at Stansted Airport. Vicky and David were now living in their own house at Highlands Park Estate on the island and it was decided that they would accommodate Ludovic, especially as he was very interested in spending time at the riding stables and would need to make an early start in the mornings with Vicky. Anas, the other French teenager would not arrive until the 2nd of July, a month later, and he would be staying at our house.

Unfortunately, after a few weeks, Ludovic proved to be too challenging with his behaviour for Vicky and David to have him staying there full time, so he ended up living with us at Rosebank Road. He could be a really nice person most of the time, but there were times when he could be inconsiderate and selfish, like the day he just decided to take Will's skateboard without asking permission, removing the wheels and painting it a different colour. Will was so angry that he nearly hit him, which was not like Will at all.

The times that Ludovic seemed to be at his best was when he was at the stables helping with the horses and being rewarded with a riding lesson. When he heard that there was a horse show coming up and that he would be able to enter one of the classes, provided he behaved like a gentleman, he really did begin to work hard all round.

With only three days to go before the horse show, the girls gave Ludovic a smart outfit, including a hard top bowler hat. He was so excited to be going to the show. He had never taken part in anything like that before and could not wait to try on his outfit. He would be showing Ben as 'Horse in Hand'. The sitting room door opened, and in walked Ludovic dressed in his complete show day outfit. He looked so arrogantly smart that in my mind I had him already earmarked for a prize.

* * *

The day of The Five Parishes Horse Show arrived. Kim, Vicky, and other helpers had all put a lot of work into the preparation of the horses and tack, including smart and correct show dress.

Everyone arrived at the stables early to allow time to check that all was ready for the day that they had prepared so hard for. The horsebox would need to take two separate trips, as they were taking four horses for the day. Jenny and Treacle went with Ludovic and Ben, then Kim and Laura with Vicky and Shelley.

This was just the beginning of the day. We would be meeting the rest of the family at the show, which was being held on land known as Fingringhoe Ranges. I do not think that anyone could have predicted a day with so many unforeseen events. Alan had returned to the stables at East Mersea to collect Kim, who was waiting to get the last two horses into the trailer. David, Charlotte and George had joined the family gathering, together with Smudge and Chloe.

The entertainment for the day was to be more than just the horse show. It was advertised as The Five Parishes Show and had been running since August 1932, only suspended during the Second World War. There were marquees full of exhibitors, home produce and crafts, with various types of stalls and

CHAPTER 44

interactive activities. There was also going to be a dog show, so I think I can honestly say there was something to interest everyone.

The various events with the horses would be spread out over the day. Kim had already taken part in one jumping event. Laura was grazing quietly, when suddenly a low-flying helicopter passed overhead, terrifying her and making her rear up. David grabbed the reins and tried to calm the situation. She reared up again. I stood there feeling very anxious. David then moved his hand in front of her eyes, which certainly seemed to have a calming effect. He then moved his head close to Laura, staring into her eyes. It was as though she had suddenly been hypnotised. She went absolutely calm. David then massaged the inside of her ear, which made her so relaxed that she rolled over onto the grass. Kim was chatting to some friends, unaware of what had taken place. When she returned, she was surprised to see Laura lying in the grass, with David sitting beside her. I could not believe that David had suddenly produced this hidden talent.

Vicky was helping to get Ludovic and Ben ready for the Horse in Hand event. There were sixteen entries in this class, and we were all hoping that he would be able to take a prize home to France. We all gathered to watch the event and I am pleased to say that he won third prize – it was well deserved.

The time came for the next event with Kim and Laura: another jumping event. Kim had managed to clear three jumps. The fourth jump was just coming up. All seemed to be going well, when suddenly Laura refused the jump. The horse edged to the side, throwing Kim, who was dragged along the ground with her foot tangled in the stirrup, causing injury to her leg.

Jenny, one of the youngest members of the family to be competing in the jumping event, riding Treacle, had also completed three jumps. Suddenly, as they approached the next jump, Treacle began to seriously play up, throwing Jenny to the ground and causing what appeared to be an injury to her shoulder.

It was reckoned by some of the competitors that the helicopter that had flown over the showground had played a part in unsettling some of the horses before their events took place. Thankfully, St John's Ambulance volunteers were present and it was recommended that both Kim and Jenny should attend the hospital for a check-up. I will never forget seeing them both being taken off – at least they were able to support each other. Meanwhile, there were four horses to get home to the stables, needing to be fed and watered.

Both Kim and Jenny were released from hospital later that evening. Jenny had a dislocated shoulder and Kim had torn ligaments and tendons in her ankle. It took them at least two months to get over their injuries, but it did not put them off riding in any way.

CHAPTER 44

CHAPTER 45

Goodbye John

OVERLEAF: *John Farthing.*
ABOVE: *(Top) The family enjoy a day at the beach hut, from left:*
Chloe, Pixie, Kim, Andy, Dudley, Will, Kate, Alan, Sophie,
Ralph, Vicky; Pixie and Alan.

I had always wanted to own a beach hut, but this had never been on Alan's wish list. In fact, I knew I would have a difficult time persuading him, as he thought they were a waste of money. Then, in 1996, I got to hear of a hut for sale that was very reasonably priced. It was in a nice area along Victoria Esplanade, near the car park and children's play area. We could park the car directly behind the hut, which was absolutely ideal. When I told Alan about it he wasn't exactly impressed with the idea, but he agreed to go and view it. I went and collected the key and once we got inside, we both realised why it was cheap. There was an awful lot of work to be done, but everything inside was going to be left: deckchairs, heater, gas cooker/oven, beach toys and a large old antique pine chest of drawers – all included in the price of the hut for £350. I wanted it so badly, but Alan didn't. He thought that there was too much work to be done.

In the end, I more or less got my own way. We did a deal. I would pay for the hut and he would get some help and do the repairs. I was so excited. I would now be the owner of a beach hut.

Firstly, the hut had to be cleared of all the trash and treasure – yes, there was one item that turned out to be a treasure! I sent the old pine chest to Reeman and Dansie's auction rooms and it made £150. I was delighted. However, once everything had been removed, we became aware of how much repair work had to be done. My brother John's advice was to "pull the bugger down and erect a new one."

GOODBYE JOHN

John had various jobs over the years, including working for Hill's, the builders, and eventually opening up a building business in Halstead with another tradesman. They named the business H+R Stroods and began trading along the Mersea Road at Blackheath, Colchester. Lee Tyler became a partner in the business which specialised in the renovation of old pubs.

At that stage, John showed great kindness in looking to employ members of the family. Sophie did a degree in languages from 1987 to 1990 at Essex University and then returned in 1990 and 1991 to study computing. This came in useful when she went to work for Uncle John, doing all the computerised accounts. Alan did the manual bookkeeping. John's brother, Tim, also worked there, as did John's son, Mark. Apparently, there were some hilarious arguments that went on between them and 'the boss.' Alan retired in 2004 and Sophie went to work at Colchester Museums. Stroods still continues under the leadership of Lee Tyler on the island.

* * *

The fact that John owned his own building business in 1996 meant that he could offer us a really good deal on building a brand new beach hut. He would get the necessary materials at cost price and we would only pay the cost of the men's wages. It turned out to be a fantastic buy and gave so much pleasure to all the family and friends. We played croquet on the grass in front of the hut, as it was on the back row and had the advantage of the grass in front. In only a few strides, you were on the sandy beach with the opportunity for swimming in the sea.

For the next sixteen years it served the family well, but after that we felt that we had all grown out of our hut. We sold it on to a local man who was in my class at school many years ago,

CHAPTER 45

when it was still called West Mersea County Primary School. We sold the hut for £10,000 in 2012. Today, in 2021, beach huts along Victoria Esplanade are priced at £45,000.

I must say at this point how much Alan enjoyed his times there: relaxing with a book, playing cricket with the children, on occasions fishing off the beach and sometimes just doing nothing at all. A far cry from having to persuade him it was a good idea. We wouldn't have had those lovely sixteen years if it weren't for John's kindness in helping build the new hut.

***

It was the middle of July 1998 and John had been fighting cancer for quite a long time. He was now in hospital and I think we all realised how seriously ill he was. At only fifty-two years old, this did not seem fair. We all loved him so much.

A week had passed and it would soon be James' and Vicky's birthdays. James' was on the 28th and Vicky's was the 29th of July. I prayed that he would not leave us on either of those days. My prayers were answered, and he sadly fell asleep on the 30th of July. Alan was our hidden strength and we all managed to get through our sorrow and laugh about the good times we had with John.

It was a wonderful day for his final send off. The sun shone and there was a warm breeze in the air. Family and friends began to arrive at the house, ready to follow the two large horses with black plumes and the beautiful carriage carrying John on his last journey along Mersea Avenue into the village. Three proud sons, Andrew, Mark and Gary, walked slowly behind the carriage. John's two brothers, Terry and Tim, joined them for the last two hundred yards to the church. John's wife Rene followed, full of love at this sad time.

After the emotional service, they journeyed along Coast Road. The tide was high and the sun glistened on the water as dear John was taken to his resting place in Firs Road cemetery.

Over a hundred people arrived back at John and Rene's home to celebrate his life in their beautiful garden. There were lots of amusing tales of the past being told. Dare I mention that, on this sad day, there was also lots of laughter – but that is what John did. He always made us laugh and he laughed a lot himself. He will never be forgotten.

CHAPTER 45

CHAPTER 46

Strictly not ballroom

OVERLEAF: *John Douglas and the JD Band, from left: James Weaver, David Unwin, John Douglas, Ray Hailey, Bill Dyer.*

Towards the end of the 1990s, when James was playing in a very popular country band called John Douglas and the JD Band, I became interested in line dancing after attending some of their gigs and watching all of the dancers enjoying themselves. I had a chat with Pam Hailey, the drummer's wife, who told me about a weekly line dance class that took place in a hall in Braintree that was part of the Lake and Elliot's Social Club. This was to open up a whole new social life for me.

Alan agreed to drive there for the first session so that I could get used to finding the way. There were no 'sat navs' in those days. Pam agreed to meet us at the venue.

We arrived early and were introduced to Sandra and Bill Barker, who were the parents of the talented young dance instructor, Fabian Barker. Fabian had two attractive female helpers, who demonstrated the steps before the start of the dance. When the music began to play, they joined the dancers so that we had someone to follow. One would dance at the back of the hall and one in the middle, which was very helpful for beginners to copy. Dancing was not exactly Alan's scene, but he was happy to sit and listen to the country music and get a drink from the bar.

After the first week of dance, I drove my own car there, together with Sophie and two extra passengers – Alan's sister, Josie, who was already into country music and line dancing, and my friend Vera Samuels, who lived in Wigborough. We had an enjoyable evening. It started a new interest and it was a totally different dance style to the more traditional style of ballroom dance that I was used to.

* * *

One evening, on our way home from Braintree, when there was just me and Sophie in the car, the weather changed from being pleasant to strong winds, heavy rain, thunder and lightning. The rain became so bad that the roads were flooding. We were on the A120. I knew we had to pull over. If lorries were stopping, then I must stop also. Sophie's wheelchair was in the boot. It was impossible to even consider getting out. We stayed for what seemed an age.

I then turned to Sophie and said,

"Sophie, shall we try and make a move or would you prefer to hang on a bit longer?"

"Let's go, Mum. I'm getting cold," she replied.

After three tries, the car started and we were on the way home, sometimes having to stop because of the flooding. I thought I was being so careful with my driving, but suddenly a large lorry overtook us at speed, throwing water all over the windscreen. This momentarily took away our visibility, until the wipers were able to do their job.

We decided to avoid our usual journey home through the back roads and to stay on the main road through to Colchester instead. At last, we were on the main Mersea road approaching Pete Tye Common, when Sophie suddenly said,

"Mum did you check whether there would be a high tide before we left home this evening?"

"No, I didn't, but we'll soon find out."

After the horrendous journey we'd just encountered all we wanted to do was to get back home. But, being an islander, it's sometimes the case that you forget to 'check the tide'. It can be a heart sinking moment as you approach the Strood to see the queue of traffic waiting for the tide to go down.

CHAPTER 46

As we approached The Peldon Rose pub, I could see there was indeed a queue of cars. But, to our delight, they were slowly on the move. Hopefully, the tide was on the way out, which would mean we should soon be home and dry!

Once we arrived on Mersea, we could see that there hadn't been anywhere near as much rain as the amount we had encountered on our drive, but this is so often the case on the island.

CHAPTER 47

A *family wedding* and a new millenium

OVERLEAF: *Vicky and Alan at Rosebank Road.*
ABOVE: *(Top) Ten bridesmaids, five pageboys, and a wedding; Vicky, David and 'Shelley'; Alan and Pixie in fancy dress, celebrating the new millenium.*

Vicky and David eventually got married on Saturday, the 9th of October 1999 at The Assembly Hall, East Road, West Mersea. Vicky had spent some happy times at Sunday School there, as did her brothers and sisters.

The ceremony was conducted by Mr Peter French. I think it was probably one of the largest weddings that had been held in the chapel. We had a large supportive family and friends, as well as David's large family, so it was not surprising that there were ten bridesmaids and five young pageboys – we couldn't leave any of the young children out.

The bride and ten bridesmaids all began to arrive at our house in Rosebank Road, ready to get dressed in their pretty clothes. They had their hair arranged by Kim, who had qualified as a hairdresser at college, and my sister-in-law Shirley, who was also a hairdresser. The five young pageboys all arrived already smartly dressed in their outfits. I cannot say that at this stage everything went smoothly. There was laughter and arguments among the youngsters and one in tears, but it all came together in the end.

Christine (Chrissie), my close friend and a professional photographer, came to take some pre-wedding photographs at the house and some outside in Miss Snell's garden, across the road. Miss Snell had a lovely lawn and the background scenery was good, which would add to the quality of the pictures. David's Dad also took some photographs.

The white stretch limo pulled into Rosebank Road and the first bridesmaids got into the car. I would be travelling next with the remaining bridesmaids and pageboys. We all felt very privileged, driving through the village in the long, white, posh car.

It was a lovely ceremony. I will always remember Alan dressed in his top hat and tails walking up the aisle with Vicky on his arm in her beautiful wedding gown, followed by her entourage.

At the end of the ceremony when everyone was waiting outside and more photographs were being taken, Vicky was suddenly faced with a big surprise – her horse, Shelley, arrived as a good luck charm. The next surprise to everyone was seeing Vicky mount Shelley in her long, white wedding gown. It made a pretty and unusual picture. After many assorted photos had been taken, the guests made their way to the reception at the Two Tides Club, Seaview Avenue.

The wedding breakfast was followed by the usual speeches. Alan did really well with no specially prepared speech, but whatever he said at the time caused loads of laughter among the guests. The evening presented two lots of entertainment. Firstly, some disco music, followed by live music from Skandal, the band James was in. A good time was had by all – a very memorable day.

***

The next family celebration was for the new millennium and everyone was invited to go to Vicky and David's house. James was working with Skandal, but Maggie, Jenny, Holly and Jack were able to attend with the rest of the Weavers and the Bleezes. Everyone dressed up in fancy dress and some challenging games had been organised by (I think) Jo Bleeze, David's mum. There are some amusing photos to be seen.

After a few years of being married, Vicky and David began to realise that their relationship was becoming problematic. However hard they tried, they could not make things work.

CHAPTER 47

Sadly, the only way forward was to sell the house and get a divorce. The sale of the house allowed them to both buy their own properties.

This was a situation that neither Alan, nor myself, ever expected to see happen. Our two granddaughters lived with their mum, but spent time with their dad when possible. David was a good dad, but most of the responsibility was with Vicky, and, of course, Alan and I were always there with backup support when needed.

Eventually, Vicky fell in love again with Alistair Burns, known to everyone as Ralph. They were married at The Registry Office in Colchester on Wednesday, the 23rd of February 2011. It was a lovely day. Alan and I were so pleased to see Vicky find happiness again, and knew they would be a good partnership.

CHAPTER 48

The haunted house

OVERLEAF: *Kim and Andy with young Dudley.*
ABOVE: *Charlotte holds baby Harry.*

Sadly, Kim's relationship with her partner, Andrew (Smudge), was not working well enough to keep them together, although they did try to work things through for Chloe, their lovely young daughter. However, Kim eventually ended up renting a rather nice flat for herself and Chloe at the bottom of Empress Avenue, facing onto Victoria Esplanade and with a lovely view looking across the sea.

Eventually, Kim met and fell in love with Andy and by August 2001 they were together and living as a family. Five years later, in June 2006, Kim and Andy welcomed their son Dudley into the world. Chloe loved having a little brother. They were a proper little family unit.

While Kim was pregnant, Charlotte found out she was pregnant too. She was only seventeen at the time. It was a worrying time for Vicky as she knew how difficult it could be being a young mum. We sat down with Charlotte to discuss her options, but at the end of the day it was her decision. She decided she wanted to keep the baby, rather than have any regrets later on. In November, she gave birth to a son. She was very proud to show us all her little boy, Harry.

* * *

By the time Chloe was in her teens and Dudley was about four years old, Kim and Andy were looking for somewhere else to live, preferably with a nice garden for Dudley to play in. They were made aware of a really nice house in Estuary Park Road, which was up for rent. After viewing from the outside, the whole property and garden looked inviting and they decided to go ahead and view inside. The property was appealing enough for them to make the decision to go ahead and rent it. Once Alan and I realised exactly which property it was, we were sure that it had previously been built and owned by Mr Cock, a local builder on the island.

The day arrived when the move took place and all the family was happy for them. However, the excitement of living there was short-lived, as strange things began to happen in the house that could not be explained. It all began with the lights suddenly turning themselves on. The hot water heater would switch off by itself and the garage door opened randomly. Young Dudley suddenly had an imaginary friend, who would sit at the end of his bed and Dudley would position toys in the wardrobe for him to play with. This was all becoming very worrying for the family to handle. Cupboard doors would suddenly bang from the inside. The draining board on the kitchen sink seemed to have been thumped from underneath, sending plates crashing down on the drainer.

What with smoke detectors going off on their own at night and taps turning themselves on, it was all beginning to become too much to cope with. The only explanation they could come up with was that they were living in a haunted house.

This had been going on for far too long. The whole scenario became quite worrying, as all logical explanations had been ruled out. We wanted them to leave the property right away and come and live with us until a more suitable property could be found. Kim and Andy agreed gladly to our suggestion and returned to Rosebank Road. It was lovely to have a full house again.

CHAPTER 48

CHAPTER 49

Sophie goes gallivanting

OVERLEAF: *Charlotte and Sophie meet chef James Martin.*
ABOVE: *(Top) Sophie in Croatia with Dejan and Zeljka Susic;*
Sophie addressing conference delegates in Belgrade, Serbia.

Sophie had been faced with various problems during her younger years, but always managed to overcome them and never seemed to look back – except to recall some of her adventurous holidays and the good times.

Charlotte, our granddaughter and Sophie's niece, was now a very sensitive, down-to-earth teenager, who often spent time with Sophie as her helper. Sophie had promised Charlotte that when she was sixteen they would go on holiday together. Never did I dream that it would be a Mediterranean Cruise.

On the 25th of August 2004 we were making our way to Stansted Airport with a car full of luggage that included two wheelchairs, two suitcases and four passengers. The reason for two wheelchairs was that the motorised wheelchair gave Sophie more independence, whilst the manual was more flexible in small spaces.

Once we arrived at the airport, I began to feel nervous knowing the responsibility that was facing Charlotte – two wheelchairs and all their luggage. I need not have worried as Charlotte is a very resourceful person.

The flight was from Stansted airport to Palma, Majorca, where they boarded the ship. On the 26th of August, the first stop was Tunisia. They did not get off the ship at this stage, as it was too difficult and not necessarily recommended for two young women to go into the town alone. However, there was plenty of varied entertainment on board for those that did not want to leave the ship. The evenings provided entertainment that covered all tastes, with music, singing and dancing.

The 27th of August took them to Rome, Italy, where they enjoyed visiting the Vatican and Colosseum. On the 28th of August, they moved on to Sestri Levante and by the 29th of August, they had reached St Tropez and St Raphael, France. The 30th of August, saw their arrival at Barcelona in Spain. That evening, the girls were pleased to meet Chef James Martin and have a chat with him before eating in his restaurant aboard the ship.

Their last day, the 31st of August, was at Palma, Majorca, where they had a couple of hours free to look around before going to the airport, ready to fly home. At the airport the girls were slightly anxious, as the manual wheelchair had got a puncture and the battery was very low on the motorised chair. As there was a flight delay, it was uncertain whether the battery would last. It was lucky for the girls that the battery did hold out until they arrived at Stansted. Alan and I were anxiously waiting for them to show up.

"Here they come," said Alan.

They were being accompanied by a member of staff because of the problems with the wheelchairs. At this stage we were able to take over, glad to have them home safe and sound.

* * *

Because of the excellent work that was being done on disability access at Colchester Museums, Sophie was asked to speak at a conference in Belgrade, Serbia. This trip would have a more serious purpose than her last trip with Charlotte. It was an event funded by the British Council. Sophie was both excited and proud to be invited to undertake this work. On this occasion, Abi, one of her personal assistants, was happy to travel abroad and work with her.

The plane journey was booked at Stansted Airport and Alan, as usual, was able and happy to be the 'Taxi Driver'. I also happily went on the journey, because I loved a ride out

CHAPTER 49

and a meal at the airport restaurant before coming home.

The day before the actual conference, Sophie and Abi went on a specially arranged tour of the historic sites, seeing the places that were hard hit by the conflict between Serbia and Croatia. Even though the war had ended ten years previously, there were still buildings that remained shells and in ruins. Despite their problems, the people were very proud of their heritage and how they had survived so much.

After the conference, Sophie attended an evening reception in the company of the British Ambassador to Serbia.

* * *

As the success of her work at Colchester Museums continued, Sophie was invited abroad once again, this time to Zagreb, Croatia. She was asked to run a two-day seminar and deliver workshops. This time, Rosie Long was to be Sophie's personal assistant and she was looking forward to the new challenge of working abroad.

The organiser of the seminar, Zeljka Susic, ensured all the arrangements for meals and accommodation were taken care of for Sophie. During her stay, she was also treated to sightseeing trips of notable places in the area. Zeljka and her husband took her to the Plitvice Lakes, a UNESCO World Heritage Site, as well as the pretty seaside city of Zadar. Zeljka and her husband, Dejan, went out of their way to make it a memorable trip and they have remained in contact ever since.

CHAPTER 50

Dancing girls

OVERLEAF: *(Left to right) Pixie, Linda Sterry, Jackie Long, Josie Hegerty;*
ABOVE: *(Top) From left – Mary Drake, Pixie, Linda Sterry, Josie Hegerty; Pixie, Charlotte and Jack receive their line dancing certificates of achievement; Stephen Rice and Sophie at the screening of their short film Between the Wars.*

Even more fun opportunities opened up for me when I joined Debbie Millar's School of Dance doing line dancing at Ardleigh Village Hall. The weekly regulars from Mersea Island were my sister-in-law, Josie Hegerty, and two good friends, sisters Linda Sterry and Jackie Long.

Debbie was a professional teacher of ballet, tap, modern, theatre and disco, to name a few, so our line dancing class was to be taken seriously – but not to the extent that we did not enjoy a good laugh.

After a period of serious teaching, Debbie announced that we were good enough to perform to an audience. This caused laughter from some of the dancers, but Debbie assured us that she had taken bookings for us to perform. Most of our class were used to performing in front of people and said it was a rewarding experience. We began in the summer months, performing at garden parties and summer shows. It was so encouraging listening to the applause, knowing that we were appreciated.

The biggest accolade was the time we performed on stage in the famous Princes Theatre in Clacton in 2005. The show was produced and directed by Debbie and titled, A Journey Through The Year. It was a fantastic show of music, dancing and singing with over one hundred and thirty-six performers.

The fourteen line dancers took on the part of World War Two Land Girls. We were all dressed in the sort of outfits that were worn by the girls in the Land Army. They did vary slightly, depending on the actual work which was being undertaken on the farms at the time. I was particularly lucky to have the real thing with my outfit, as Sophie was working as an access officer for The Colchester Museums Service. She decided to ask Mike, a member of staff and World War Two fanatic, if he had anything in his large collection to do with the Land Army. Luckily, he had a complete original outfit, including a hat, tie, blouse, and trousers. Debbie was impressed when I turned up with my rare acquisition.

The dress rehearsals at the theatre made us all feel rather nervous when on stage, looking into the auditorium at the vast amounts of seats, which would be filled up by the audience. We had heard that there were only a few seats left – it was going to be a sell out!

Our good friends, Fred and Heather Pargeter, with two of their young children, Beth and Archie, had booked seats next to Alan, Sophie and George. When Alan first saw me dressed in the clothes I was going to perform in, he started to grin and soon began to chuckle loudly.

"What's the matter, Alan?" I asked

"Nothing dear. It's just the way things looked back in those days with wartime clothes on the farm."

I ran upstairs and looked at myself in the full-length wardrobe mirror and I could understand his laughter.

Now, on the evening of the big show, when all the fourteen Land Girls, including myself and the three other Mersea girls, danced to the music of Glenn Miller's song, In The Mood, we put all of our energy into the dance. We enjoyed the magic and atmosphere of the loud applause from an appreciative audience. Apparently, Alan enjoyed our performance so much that he laughed until tears rolled down his cheeks. To be honest, I think he saw the hat and baggy trousers I was wearing, together with some of the other outfits, as pretty laughable. Our granddaughter, George said,

"Grandad laughed until he cried."

At least he enjoyed it and we also enjoyed being in

CHAPTER 50

Debbie Millar's show, which was a huge success – something everyone in the show could be proud of. George loved the show so much that she wanted to attend Debbie's classes.

I was able to enrol George for dancing classes with Debbie. At the time, she was twelve years old and did modern dance and disco, which she both enjoyed and seemed to do really well at. In fact, by February 2007, the family were again at The Princes Theatre in Clacton, ready to watch a show called A Tribute To The Musicals.

George danced in two numbers: a disco dance entitled Time Warp, where the girls all wore bright spiky orange wigs with attractive outfits, and a modern dance called Singing In The Rain with light blue leotards, and, of course, umbrellas. This was another great successful show, enjoyed by a great audience. Who would have thought that watching Nan line dance would lead to George dancing to a large audience at The Princes Theatre!

* * *

George's mum and Auntie Kim also had their own memories of the world of performing arts. The Fourth Protocol was a British Cold War film featuring Michael Caine and Pierce Brosnan, based on the novel written by Frederick Forsyth. During the making of the film there was an advert seeking extras in the Maldon area, where part of the filming would be taking place. Kim, Vicky and their friend Julie Hopper promptly applied at the Job Centre in Colchester. Luckily, they were all selected and were very proud to be able to participate in a blockbuster film!

They travelled from Mersea to Colchester by bus and then they were collected by a coach which took them to Maldon. Kim became friendly with Paul McKenzie and, on one occasion, had a lift on his motorbike. They were paid very well at a rate of fifty pounds per day and there was a large catering van providing a good selection of foods. They attended the filming for a few days and on one of the days the girls were lucky enough to see Michael Caine. The film was released on the 28th of August 1987.

* * *

Sophie also had her own creative success. During the 90s, she started collaborating on writing film scripts with family friend, Stephen Rice. They worked well together, both coming up with ideas to work on, sometimes for a full length feature film, other times just short films. On this occasion, it was an idea for a short film that got them writing. During the 90s, the Balkans experienced great conflicts, with people fleeing to safety. At times, it led to negative reactions towards refugees.

In the short film, called Between The Wars, Stephen and Sophie explored the attitudes and reactions towards people who have been part of conflict. Their story brings together a World War II veteran and a survivor of the Balkans conflict. While there was initial tension between them, they become reconciled through their recognition of both having experienced war, conflict and prejudice.

The script was entered into a competition, where the prize was to have the winning script actually produced into a short film. Stephen and Sophie had to attend an awards evening where the winner would be announced. It was a very special evening, knowing they had been shortlisted and were in with a chance of winning. To their delight, their script won.

Everything was then put in motion by the production company and over the following months the film was made. A couple of times Stephen and Sophie were lucky enough to go on set and watch it coming to life.

The film premiered at the Curzon Cinema in London, which Stephen and Sophie attended. It was quite an evening seeing their film on the big screen for the first time. Once the film was released, it was entered for the BAFTAs in the Best Short Film category. Again, the film was shortlisted, but this time did not reach the final selections. They were, nevertheless, very proud of their achievement.

A split-second action

OVERLEAF: *Vicky, pictured around the time of the incident.*

On the 24th of March 2007, Vicky and some of her friends decided to have a night of enjoyment at The Escape Nightclub in Copford (formerly Kings, and prior to that, The Windmill). Chloe also decided, at the last minute, that she could also do with a night out. Our fostered teenager had gone off with some friends for the evening and she had promised not to be late home. Alan and I decided to have fish and chips and a quiet night in front of the television.

However, as usual, things did not go as planned. By eleven o'clock, our young person was still not home. She had promised to be in by ten thirty. We decided to give it until eleven thirty before notifying the police and Social Services. At eleven thirty, there was still no call or message, so we notified the police, who arrived within twenty minutes of our phone call. Looking after problematic teenagers meant that having the police in for a chat was quite a common occurrence.

During the time that the two policemen were taking down notes about our missing person, they received a telephone call regarding some trouble at The Escape nightclub. They apologised for leaving in a hurry, but would get in touch if there was anything else that they needed to know.

After the police had left, I looked at Alan and said,

"Alan, I'm really worried about Vicky and Chloe and their mates."

"Oh? Why's that then?" he replied.

"Because they're in the same nightclub that the police were called to because of an incident."

A SPLIT-SECOND ACTION

"For goodness sake, Pix, stop worrying. There are probably hundreds of people at the club. Why think the worst?"

Vicky, Chloe and their friends had been enjoying their evening. They were on the dance floor happily dancing, when Vicky was accidentally burnt on her arm by a female who was holding a lighted cigarette while dancing. Automatically, and in pain, Vicky moved her arm which caused her to nudge another person dancing on the crowded dance floor.

At that stage, things got out of hand and Vicky was glassed in the face with a champagne glass. Adrenalin and fear made Vicky want to protect herself. The liquid that was running down her face wasn't alcohol from the broken glass, but blood from the injury she sustained. It took three security men to keep Vicky safe. An ambulance was called and Vicky was taken to hospital for treatment. Eventually, a taxi was called to bring the nightclubbers back to Mersea Island.

Vicky had small slivers of glass removed from her face. Instead of stitches, a decision was made to glue her skin, which worked very well. We were not made aware of all the drama until the following morning, as they 'did not want to worry us'. It was strange how I got that feeling of worry after the police had left the house. Thankfully, our young person also returned home the next day.

Four months later, a court heard how Victoria Bleeze had a champagne glass pushed into her face after trouble flared in a nightclub near Colchester. Her attacker told police that she could not remember very much, as she had been drinking. A judge at Chelmsford Crown Court said her behaviour had been 'loutish'. However, she was spared jail "by a whisker".

Judge David Turner QC gave her a twelve month sentence, suspended for two years, plus a two-hundred-hour, unpaid work order. She was also ordered to pay Vicky £1,500.00 compensation and £395.00 costs. Clare Ashcroft, mitigating, said the guilty person had acted totally out of character and references showed that she was very well thought of.

CHAPTER 51

Miss Ashcroft said her client was very sorry and had never before shown any aggression – "It was a split-second action."

Frank

It was after the completion of my first book, From When I Can Remember, that many people either wrote or telephoned me to say how much they had enjoyed reading about Mersea Island and its secrets, and also the stories of the Farthing family.

One of the telephone calls led me to arrange a visit to see Frank Farthing and his wife, Irene, who believed they were related to me. Alan Smith, my cousin, who had been researching the Farthing and Smith families, was also keen to meet some more of the Farthings. His grandfather was Alan G Farthing – known as 'Manny' – the dairyman. My cousin Alan travelled from Leicestershire to West Mersea and we set off to Tillingham in Essex, where Frank and Irene now lived.

We left the island on the 28th of August 2008, curious to know what we would learn about the Farthing family descendents, who had decided to leave Mersea Island many years ago. Arriving at the address in the pretty little village of Tillingham, we were met at the door by an elderly man, who introduced himself as Frank, and his wife, Irene. We were invited indoors, where we then met Frank's brother, John, and his wife, June.

It was strange and exciting for us to learn that our three grandfathers, Travers (Trav), Alan (Manny) and James (Jim) were indeed brothers, born at Cross Farm, Cross Lane, West Mersea to Sophia and William Farthing, parents of thirteen brothers and sisters.

Talking about the family and looking at various

FRANK

photographs, the time passed very quickly and we decided
it was time for lunch at the local pub, The Fox and Hounds,
which was only a short distance away. After a pleasant lunch,
we all returned to Frank's home. It was while we were looking
at some more photographs that a strange thing happened.
My interest was instinctively drawn to a particular picture
of a good-looking lad, lying among the other photographs
on the table.

"Who's this?" I asked, picking up the photograph and
looking at it more closely.

"That's Geoffrey, my older brother, who sadly drowned
when he was only fifteen years old," answered Frank.

I knew that this had to be the young relation who had
tragically drowned somewhere in the Southend area many
years ago. It was undoubtedly the loss of Geoffrey that had
prompted our parents to give us a warning:

*"Never go swimming until an hour after eating food. You
could get cramp and drown."*

This warning – and the consequences – had been drummed
into all of us as children.

I was now interested to know more about the circumstances
that had led to his death, but did not like to ask questions.
However, at this point, Frank started to tell us the sad story of
the day his brother Geoffrey drowned in the River Crouch.

"Our mother was away on holiday. It was the first time she
had ever had the opportunity to actually go away. The family
were managing fairly well with our father's help, until the day
that Geoffrey went off to work at the timber yard, Davey and
Armitage, on Wallasea Island. He left for work early, taking his
packed lunch. The morning was very hot and the workmen had
all been busy. They were ready for their lunch break. Geoffrey
quickly ate his sandwiches and, being a good athlete and
strong swimmer, ran along the sea wall and dived into Lion
Creek. Suddenly, he appeared to get into difficulties. His friends
desperately tried to save him, but sadly his life was lost. It was

CHAPTER 52

322

the 25th of July 1949. The reason given for the drowning was that he developed cramp through swimming with a full stomach."

Frank walked off into another room, returning after a short while holding an old red leather purse.

"This is the only thing my brother left."

Frank opened the purse and tipped the contents into his hand. There were some tarnished half-crowns (12½p) and a few coppers. This inheritance of Frank's had been tucked away for decades, but for me it still held some powerful energy, a memory of the past. I was taken back to the sadness of what had now gone, but which for the family was never forgotten.

It was time for us to return to Mersea Island. Our day had been enjoyable and rewarding – sharing the past with our relations and catching up with the present. We said our goodbyes, promising to meet up in the future. As we turned the corner at the end of the road, I could still see them waving goodbye. We drove in silence for a while. I think we were both thinking about the events of the day and, for me personally, I still felt the sadness at the loss of the young Geoffrey Farthing.

FRANK

A bank robbery

OVERLEAF: *(Left to right) A previous police station/house on High Street North; the last police station on the Island on East Road; PC Ron Beckwith on patrol along Victoria Esplanade with Empress Ave in the background (before Orchid Field Court flats were built); outside Barclays bank at the time of the robbery; Jim Pullen-Appleby.*
ABOVE: *Local Bobbies of the '70s/'80s (back row) Dick Scholar, Phil Passfield, John Bolingbroke, Ian Crossley; (front row) Jeff Cox (Rowhedge), Det. Constable Peter Ballard, Sgt Reg Shelly, Mick Aitchison (Birch).*

Policing on the island has seen big changes over the years. I have been lucky enough to experience a few decades. I recently found out that the very first policeman on Mersea Island was William Frances, in 1844, and he was twenty-two years old. He arrived during November and the population was only nine hundred.

Apart from the first policeman in 1844, there is not a lot of history to be told until the 1900s. Although they go way back to the medieval period, The Court Rolls of the Manor of East Mersea still exist, and indicate the normal local matters: from poaching and damage to hedges to non-payment of tithes and disputes. Of course, there are many tales of smuggling going on until around the nineteenth century. It is rumoured that smugglers would often store their contraband in the pond by the Peldon Rose Pub.

Many of the Mersea locals will only be able to remember the police station in East Road, but there was a police house prior to this in the early 1900s in High Street North. It was part of Reymead Terrace. I can remember this being in use up until the early 1950s. I can also remember PC Andrews being there, because he caught me riding my bike after dark without lights. He stopped me and said,

"You're Pixie Farthing."

I answered,

"Yes, that's right."

Then he said,

"Well, get off that bike and walk home, otherwise I'll be

A BANK ROBBERY

coming round to see your Dad."

I didn't want the police to visit our house, so I made sure I walked all the way home.

PC Liggins also lived in Reymead Terrace Police House, High Street North in 1948/49 and, according to some old council records going back to 1926, there was a PC Pink. The other police house in Mill Road was next door to the Methodist Church and more akin to the modern-day police station, apart from the actual police office being a shed in the garden.

I would now like to add a poem about the local police, taught to me when I was a young girl by my uncle, which was probably put together by some Mersea locals:

If you go down to the woods today,
You had better go in disguise,
If you go down in the wood today,
You're sure to get a surprise,
With ole Joe Liggins,
And Sergeant Woods,
And Major De Manby's ghost,
All are having a picnic.

In 1952 with the ever-growing population of three thousand and ten, two new police houses were built in East Road, along with the addition of a proper police station. The houses were first occupied by Sergeant Waylett and PC Nicholls.

By the 1970s and '80s, many of the locals will remember growing up with Sergeant Ian Crossley. He served our community for at least twenty-one years before he retired. Alongside him were Sergeant Butcher, PC Dave Passfield and PC Dave Wilkinson. At this time, it was common to see the local police officers on patrol. They would often be cycling around the island, managing to keep law and order very much part of the community. They were well-respected by many and perhaps feared by a few. Parents would utter words like,

CHAPTER 53

"Don't let Sergeant So-and-so catch you without lights on your bike," and we would all take notice.

It was rare for perpetrators of crime to get away with it. Reports of crime were mostly caravans being broken into on the sites and boating equipment being stolen. For more serious crimes, a roadblock would be put on the Strood. In 1993, when Sergeant Crossley retired, there were five police constables and a sergeant on the island.

There was a time when I felt personally safe and at ease, especially with our job fostering teenagers. The presence and back-up support of the police on the island helped to keep crime at bay. A phone call to Mersea Police Station would bring us help and support within five minutes. Then, during March 2011, a decision was taken to close our police station. We would now have to contact a central number where it would be decided what level of urgency the crime was that you had just reported. There had been police on Mersea Island for one hundred and seventy years. Now, with a population of seven and a half thousand, there would be no police based here at all.

* * *

On the 27ᵗʰ of May, 2009, there was an attempted bank robbery at Barclays Bank in Yorick Road.

It all happened first thing in the morning, before the bank actually opened. One of the clerks entered, ready to begin her day, when she was suddenly aware of two men being inside the building. She knew they must have gained entry through one of the back windows. One was holding what appeared to be a gun; she was absolutely terrified! One of them threatened her by saying he knew exactly where she lived. She was grabbed as she went to open the door, however, she managed to get free and get outside to where two other workers were ready to start their day's work. They all fearfully ran to Mr Cock, the butcher, for help and the police were notified immediately. They were a long time arriving, as they had to come from Colchester.

The bank clerk that was accosted by the robber had travelled to the bank in her Ford car, which was parked in the car park. Unfortunately, she must have dropped her car keys during the scuffle and the robbers made a getaway in her car, which was later found in Rushmere Close, undamaged.

Jim Pullen Appleby, a born and bred islander, was about to make a journey to Colchester, our nearest town. He was totally unaware of what had been going on in the village, until he approached the Strood causeway (the only way off the island) and saw all the police activity and a long hold-up of cars. It was then that he decided to turn round and go home. It looked as though he was going to have a long wait and he did not want to waste time queuing.

The police became suspicious of his actions when he reversed his white pick-up truck. He was pulled over, questioned and his truck was searched. Unfortunately, he had an air rifle in the back of the truck (not unusual for a Mersea man) and he was wearing a blue boiler suit, which matched the bank clerk's description.

They arrested him, which was a dramatic and frustrating event for poor innocent Jim. He was held at gunpoint by the Armed Response Unit, who were carrying machine guns. Then, he was handcuffed and taken to Colchester Police Station. After going to the custody desk, he spent all day locked up in the cells.

After being subjected to endless questions, Jim was finally released with a form to say no further action would be taken. He is a respected Mersea local who should never have been arrested and certainly not imprisoned all day. To this day, nobody has ever been caught and the crime remains unsolved. There will always be the question of whether having to wait for the police to arrive from Colchester made it easier for the perpetrators to get away. I would like to think that one day the people of Mersea will once again get their rights to have police based on the island.

CHAPTER 53

CHAPTER 54

A golden year

OVERLEAF: *A gathering of family and friends for Pixie and Alan's golden wedding anniversary.*
ABOVE: *(Clockwise from top left) Vicky and Ralph tie the knot; Will and Kate's Vegas wedding, with close friends Lou Harvey and Em Willoughby; Pixie giving Peggy cuddles; David Bleeze and Harry doting on baby Holly.*

Little did we know at the beginning of 2011 that it would be quite a year of events and celebrations.

It started with the happy event of Vicky's marriage to Ralph. We were so pleased that Vicky had finally met someone to settle down with, especially after her somewhat turbulent marriage to David. Ralph was very kind and loving to Vicky's two girls, Charlotte and George, and they had accepted him as the new man of the house.

As it was Vicky's second marriage, she didn't want a big fuss, so opted for a Registry Office wedding. There was a lovely gathering of the close families for the actual wedding and then we all returned to the Art Café at Mersea for a very memorable reception. We knew our little girl would be happy – there was another baby on the way.

By the time the wedding came around, Vicky was already six months pregnant. It was lovely that Vicky and Ralph were having a child together, as Ralph didn't have children. Charlotte and George, now grown up, were looking forward to being big sisters.

Vicky was literally blooming on the day of their wedding – the 23rd of February 2011. Looking radiant as she spoke her vows, it was lovely to see her so happy again. The day was a great time of celebration for both families.

* * *

On Saturday, the 12th of March 2011, we were going to celebrate our Golden Wedding anniversary with our five children and their partners. The actual date of our wedding was the 16th of March 1961. What we were expecting was a posh restaurant off the island. Alan had to wear a suit and tie and I was told to wear something smart, as James and Maggie had organised a surprise venue.

I was really happy about the dinner celebration, as I did not want a 'big do' because I had been lying about my age for a long time – well, not exactly lying.

Our grandchildren would ask,

"How old are you, Nan?"

I would reply by saying,

"I'm as old as my tongue and a little older than my teeth."

If their reply was,

"Are you about fifty-five, sixty?"

I would reply,

"Yes, you're about right, dear."

I didn't exactly lie, but I didn't exactly tell the truth either! Now, with a fiftieth Wedding Anniversary approaching, it wouldn't take a lot to work out my age. But it didn't happen as Alan and I expected.

Andy and Kim came to collect us, as arranged, at 7:45pm. We got in the car, both of us wondering where we were going. Andy said he needed petrol in the car and Alan said,

"You're too late for that, mate – Basil closes at 7:30 on Saturdays."

Andy then pulled over onto the forecourt of The British Legion. The double doors opened to reveal a hall full of our relations and friends. I knew it was time for us to get out of the car. This was a huge surprise, organised without us having any idea about what was going on. The family had colluded together to bring this all about.

As we walked in the doors, there were cheers, laughter and greetings from people who had travelled from many miles away. What a fantastic night we would have!

There were a variety of musical instruments waiting to be played by Café Musica – a really entertaining duo consisting of Peter Banks and our son, James. Behind the musicians was a large modern screen showing fifty years of continuous photographs of mine and Alan's life together. There was so much going on; it was hard to take it all in!

We moved round the hall, catching up with everyone. How had our five children and their families managed to get in touch with the Rawlinsons, who Alan once worked for in Hedingham, my friends from line dancing and Cousin Alan from Leicestershire?

There were many more surprises. Halfway through the evening, a buffet was produced by Gill Taylor. Alan's sister, Josie, had followed in her mother's (Nanny Weaver) cake-making and icing talents, having made a beautiful, two-tiered, iced fruit cake.

The second half of the evening saw the floor full of talented dancers, showing off many varied styles of dancing, applauded by an appreciative audience. I must mention how well-behaved the children all were and how well the hall had been decorated with plenty of balloons for the children to take home afterwards.

It had been a Golden Day all round – a day Alan and I would never forget.

* * *

Kate and Will decided to get married in Las Vegas in April 2011. They had never really felt that getting married was for them, but the idea of doing it in a place where it's hot, sunny and fun, with no pressure or hoo-ha of a regular wedding, suited them down to the ground. The year before, they had been witnesses to their good friends Em and Lou at their civil ceremony in Brighton and it probably inspired them to go for it.

So, just a few months before they set the date for their big day (Good Friday, the 22nd of April 2011), they began to think about getting organised. They asked Em and Lou if they would return the favour by going to 'Sin City' to be their witnesses. They accepted. Funnily enough, just after that, Prince William and Kate Middleton announced the date of their nuptials – thankfully, one week after our Will and Kate. We couldn't have two Will and Kates getting hitched on the same day. That would have been too confusing!

Will and Kate looked at wedding chapels and found one that they liked the look of. It was called The Little Chapel of the Flowers and was downtown, in the old part of Vegas. It also provided an online view of the service so that they could invite friends and family to watch the ceremony on the internet. Perfect! Chapel, booked; flights, booked. They also booked a post-wedding meal at The Stratosphere, a restaurant in the old town that revolved three hundred and sixty degrees. Last but not least, and with just a few weeks to spare, Will secured his suit and Kate her absolutely beautiful wedding dress.

Time to go. They got on the plane that was packed with stag and hen dos, so for about eight hours the Virgin Atlantic flight looked, sounded and smelled, for all parts, like a pub in the sky!

When they landed, they were greeted with a limo and champagne surprise organised by Em and Lou, to take them for their check-in at Caesars Palace. When you get married in Vegas, you have to get a marriage certificate from the Clark County Marriage Bureau, so when they arrived for their Easter weekend nuptials (yes, for some reason they decided to do it all in a three night city mini-break!) they went straight there to get the certificate that would allow them to get wed in the morning, live on the internet, in front of all the family and friends to whom they had sent invitations on Facebook just a few days before.

CHAPTER 54

Back at home on the island, most of the close family had arranged to go and watch the ceremony at Kim and Andy's house, as they had a big television screen that they could connect to the internet. The time difference between America and England meant we were watching it in the evening, even though the ceremony was around midday. As it got close to the time, we all got excited, gathering round the television screen. Finally, after a few technical hitches, the live feed came through and we could all see the interior of the chapel where Will and Kate were due to take their vows. A few minutes later, they came into view, Will in his smart suit and Kate in her beautiful dress. They walked up the aisle together with their two friends as witnesses. It felt wonderful to be able to view it live, even though they were thousands of miles away. The wonder of modern technology!

Alan commented in a rare emotional moment that he was missing 'young Will' as he often called him. He said it also didn't feel right that he wasn't there for his boy's big day. This was unexpected from Alan, as I was usually the one to be the softie.

The ceremony was wonderful, intimate, and Will and Kate couldn't stop grinning throughout. They were obviously very happy and enjoying their special moment. Em and Lou had front row seats, as did their online audience at home. The chap who married them was called Jerry and although it was a short ceremony, Jerry and everyone at the chapel made them feel really special, like they were the only ones getting married there that day. Knowing family and friends were watching at home still made it special for them, but without any pressure of that 'big day'. They took their vows, lit a candle, and left the chapel to Cliff Richard's song, Wired for Sound (their choice).

Straight after, the limo picked them up and drove them to the famous Welcome To Las Vegas sign where they took pictures which later got published in the wedding section on

HELLO! Magazine's website. They wandered the strip, got some pizza and a mojito cocktail, then made their way to the Stratosphere, where they enjoyed a meal as the sun set. The best thing was that they could look down and clearly see the chapel from where they were sitting.

Their honeymoon was spent in Venice: Venice, Las Vegas! They were serenaded by a nice lady as she pushed them around in a gondola in the river at the Venetian Hotel. They did some sightseeing – saw the New York New York Hotel, The Great Pyramid (The Luxor) and a touch of France at The Parisian.

As for the other Will and Kate, the Royals who got married the week after at Westminster Abbey, I hear they're still together. In fact, because of all the celebrations around their wedding, the London Eye had a special offer that our Will and Kate took advantage of upon their return from America. If you could prove you were also a married Will and Kate, you could have a free ride on the big wheel. State of Nevada marriage certificate in hand, they said yes please! To their surprise, the woman on the desk said they were one of only a few couples who did it.

They still have and use the commemorative tea towel they designed to celebrate their event. We hear a few friends still have theirs and use them too.

***

Just under a month later, on the 19th of May, Vicky and Ralph's daughter Peggy was born. She was not only little sister for George and Charlotte, but, in the weird scheme of things, an auntie to Charlotte's son Harry, who was now five years old. Our family tree was getting stranger by the minute.

Within a short space of time, Charlotte found out that she was pregnant again, with another baby due at the end of the year. Her little sister Peggy would again be an auntie by the time she was seven months old.

CHAPTER 54

Seven months later, Christmas of 2011 came along, and so did Charlotte's baby. The family members were all going to have the traditional Christmas dinner with us at Rosebank Road. Charlotte was staying with her dad and was going to come over later. As we were having our Christmas dinner, Vicky got a message on her phone. Charlotte had gone into labour and was being taken to the hospital. Vicky left her dinner and went.

The baby was obviously keen to make an appearance, as by the time Vicky got to the hospital, Charlotte had given birth to a beautiful baby girl, Holly. A perfect Christmas gift.

CHAPTER 55

A big party

OVERLEAF: *Vicky handing over her cheque to the Mary Barron Suite.*
ABOVE: *Holly in her party outfit.*

Peggy was just an eighteen-month-old baby when her mother was diagnosed with breast cancer.

I am unable to find words to describe how I felt when Vicky first told me that she had found a lump in her breast, which needed to be investigated. In September 2012, she was referred to the specialist unit at Essex County Hospital and she had immediate surgery to remove the lump, now known to be cancer. She subsequently underwent chemotherapy treatment every three weeks for four months, followed by twenty sessions of radiotherapy.

As parents and grandparents, Alan and I went through a really worrying time, but we had to keep strong to support all the family. Ralph showed so much strength and support to his new family, as George was still living at home with her Mum and also needed that extra loving support.

As Vicky began to recover, she had time to reflect on what she had been through and how she had now recovered. Being a bit of a one for parties, she planned to have a big celebration party for all her family and friends. At the same time, she wanted to raise awareness and give something back to the Mary Barron Suite at Essex County Hospital, so the celebration party quickly became a fundraising evening.

The party took place at Mersea Outdoors, previously known as East Mersea Youth Camp, a very nice venue with plenty of room for the well-known Skandal band to play. It was a fantastic party with plenty of food, dancing, singing and a huge raffle.

Vicky was now able to give back £3,000 to help the Mary Barron Suite. Generous donations had also been given by local businesses, as well as friends and relations. Presenting the cheque to the Mary Barron Suite was Vicky's way of saying a heartfelt thank you to every one of the doctors, nurses and staff who helped so much during a very difficult six months of her life. With this money, a new piece of equipment, the Accuven AV400, a handheld device, was to be purchased. This was very useful when treating young children.

Vicky was then able to return to work as Lead Support Worker at Autism Anglia, Peldon Old Road Rectory, where she had been employed since 2008.

Uncle Jack Saye

OVERLEAF: *Jack Saye bus.*
ABOVE: *A magazine clipping of Grosvenor House.*

It was while we were motoring from Mersea to Tiptree one day, that a strange and silly conversation reminded me of Uncle Jack Saye and how he had left me and the family with some amazing memories, some of which were true and some fictional.

"Where do we turn right to Tiptree?" asked Sophie.

"At Salcott traffic lights," was my reply (bearing in mind the nearest traffic light is many, many miles away), but this would have been Jack's joking answer and then he would go on to say,

"If you turn left into Salcott, you will come to the treacle mines. They've been having terrible trouble down there with woodpeckers, pecking into the wooden barrels. However, after putting sandpaper on the barrels, it blunted all their beaks and that solved the problem."

On this occasion, Sophie's friend, Wendy, was driving the car and burst into laughter, not sure which way to turn!

As we travelled to our destination in Tiptree, a few more memories of Jack's tales were told. He used to be a bus driver, driving the bus from Mersea to Colchester and back. He would also drive coach parties on various outings.

One of his tricks in days gone by, after they had all had a few drinks, was to set the windscreen wiper to the middle of the screen, with one eye to the left of the wiper and the other eye to the right. He would then line up the wiper with the middle of the road for a 'safe' ride home. That's what happened if he had drunk "far too much lotion!".

When Uncle Jack was around there would always be

moments of laughter. I can remember one day when he called in to see us. Mum asked if Auntie Nellie and the children were well and his reply was,

"Yes, mate, they're fine, but poor ole Nellie has dyed her hair and she looks just like a black Minorca!"

A black Minorca was a type of chicken. We couldn't help laughing.

"Mate, I watched her do it and it looked wassa and wassa (worse and worse) as the colour changed."

There are endless tales that Jack talked about, but a very memorable day for him was when he was only twenty years old in 1934 and Flight Lt Charles W A Scott and Captain Tom Campbell Black won the air race from England to Australia, known as The London to Melbourne Air Race. Charles Scott actually lived in West Mersea and brought about a lot of interest and support to the island.

The idea of the race was devised by the Lord Mayor of Melbourne and the prize money of £15,000 was provided by Sir Macpherson Robertson, a wealthy confectionery manufacturer, on condition that the race was named after his MacRoberston company. Today, the value of the prize money would be about £1,000,000.

The race began at RAF Mildenhall, Suffolk. The take-off date was set at dawn (6:30am) on the 20th of October 1934.

After the fantastic accolade of this great achievement, Scott organised a Flying Circus at Blue Barns Aerodrome, Ipswich Road, Colchester. Frank Cornelius, from the Mersea Cycle Shop was going to attend the Flying Circus on his motorbike and offered Jack the opportunity to ride with him as a pillion passenger. There was a competition at the event where visitors were asked to guess the altitude of various planes. Jack guessed 937 feet and was delighted when he heard he had won. The prize was a flight to Ipswich and back for two people.

Another story of Jack's was about a dark foggy night and a bus ride from Colchester to West Mersea. Jack was hardly able to drive the bus because of the thick fog. There was a large queue of people waiting in Colchester to get home and the conductor was explaining to them about the bad condition of the roads. One of the male passengers kindly offered to walk in front of the bus, with a newspaper as a guide in the darkness. When they eventually arrived at Abberton, about four miles up the road, the conductor got off the bus and collected the helpful man's bus fare, even though he hadn't even set foot on the bus!

Jack was born on Mersea Island – a proper Merseaite. There is a boat, named after him by Grandad Gasson, still sailing on the River Blackwater to this day and it is now owned by another Mersea boy, Mark Farthing – my nephew.

There is something rather comforting to know that our boating traditions still carry on through to the younger generations. Hopefully they too will pass those traditions on for generations to come.

An ever-expanding family tree

OVERLEAF: *(Top right) Marnie and brother Jacob; (top left) Holly and Amelia; (bottom left) Baby Teddy; (bottom right) Baby Grace; (far right page) left to right: Baby Amelia, Baby Jacob, Peggy, and Eliza.*
ABOVE: *George and Adam's wedding.*

In October 2015, four years after her mum Vicky had married Ralph, it was time for George's own wedding. George and Adam had been together since their teens and were well suited. It was a lovely, traditional wedding, which took place at East Mersea Church. The service was taken by Adam's grandfather, Brian Snelling, who was a vicar. George had her sisters and nieces as her bridesmaids. It was another one of those celebratory occasions that brought both families together. Even Will and his heavily pregnant wife, Kate, made the trip up from Eastbourne. The reception was held close by at Essex Outdoors, where Vicky had held her fundraising party.

Just one month later, the next happy event came along – the birth of Eliza Bea, Will and Kate's long-awaited daughter.

In February 2017, George and Adam welcomed their first child Jacob and in March, Amelia, granddaughter to James and Maggie, was born to Holly and Martyn.

In 2019, Marnie, a little sister to Jacob, came along. Later that year, Jack's son, Theodore, known as Teddy, was born on my grandfather's birthday – the 10th of May. What an incredible coincidence to be born on the birthday of your great, great, great grandad! Now that is one birthday I really shouldn't forget! The following year, in 2020, Grace arrived – a little sister for Teddy.

All in all, my ever-expanding family tree clearly needed a chapter all of its own.

Bye Al

OVERLEAF: *Our dear Al.*

ABOVE: *(From top left) Following Al on his final journey; A touching message in the snow en route; Arriving at the church; a lovely musical tribute from Bill Dyer, James and Peter Banks; Our family together in celebrating Al's life.*

It was probably during 2016 that Alan began to think twice about going on long journeys in the car. It became noticeable when we decided to go to Eastbourne for Eliza's first birthday and he said,

"I don't feel I really want to drive all that way. Don't get me wrong, I want to go, but it would be better if someone else were to do the driving."

I suggested that David Bleeze (Vicky's ex) would probably agree to drive us all in Alan's seven-seater Peugeot. David did, of course, agree to take us. Everyone had a lovely time and Alan had an easy day.

We all noticed that Alan didn't have his usual amount of energy and he did sleep quite a bit during the day. Suggestions were made that he should visit the doctor. He totally refused, saying,

"There's nothing wrong with me, only old age."

Our granddaughter, Charlotte, who had been particularly worried about her grandad, arrived at our house one day and said,

"Come on grandad, I'm taking you to the Art Café for a coffee."

Not wanting to disappoint Charlotte, he went with her.

After they had coffee, cakes and some special time together, Charlotte drove to Barfield Road and pulled up outside the clinic.

"What have you stopped here for?" asked Alan.

Charlotte replied,

"Grandad, I've booked you in for a quick medical check up."

He looked cross, but followed her inside. Only his little 'Sharlie', would have succeeded in doing this. He saw the nurse, who gave him a full medical. They arrived home looking somewhat surprised at what had happened.

That night, after going to bed, Alan had done his usual crossword and I had been reading my book. I was about to go to sleep – it was about midnight – when the phone rang. I picked it up, as it was my side of the bed. Colchester General hospital were ringing to make me aware that Mr Alan Weaver's check up at West Mersea clinic had presented them with some worrying information and they needed to investigate further. They were thinking of sending an ambulance out right away. I explained that he was in bed asleep. They said that provided he could get there first thing in the morning, it would be acceptable.

I was absolutely panic-stricken. I woke Alan and gave him the message, but he went back to sleep again. I stayed awake all night.

Alan had to stay in hospital and further tests showed that he was suffering with kidney failure. After more than a week in hospital, they were able to stabilise his condition. It was during the time of all the investigations that it was discovered that he had an aortic aneurysm. Addressing this would be put on hold until they sorted out the kidneys. He was put on medication and had a catheter fitted. He was also put on a special diet to help build him up in readiness for operating on the aneurysm. Although regular check ups showed improvements to his kidneys, it was explained that he really needed to be on dialysis.

Alan did not want to spend more than two days a week at the hospital, but realised that without the treatment he could suffer complete kidney failure. He finally agreed for the preparations to go ahead for the dialysis.

Heading up to Christmas 2017, he seemed to be improving,

CHAPTER 58

despite still being quite weak. He was warned the abdominal aneurysm was critical and they would operate as soon as he was strong enough.

We had a lovely Christmas with the whole family coming together as usual for Christmas Day and everyone gathering round at James and Maggie's in the evening. We were having a lovely time, then Alan suddenly felt unwell and returned home, with Will taking the responsibility of making his dad feel more comfortable and secure. We thought he may well have eaten too much rich food – he was on a special diet.

After a good night's rest he began to feel much better – back to his good old dry humour.

* * *

We were now well into the new year. Alan had been feeling quite well until late afternoon, when he said he had an aching pain in his stomach. He decided to take a painkiller and settle down to rest in the conservatory, which was probably his favourite room. This was where he would smoke the occasional cigarette and watch football on the television, with a cosy electric artificial coal fire that he could switch on in the winter.

Sophie was entertaining later that evening at one of Jay Stapley's 'Musical Evenings' at the MICA (Mersea Island Community Association). The tickets, as usual, were all sold out. I was going to go, but decided against it, because of Alan being unwell. Sophie looked really great, all dressed up in 1980s' gear. She made her way through from her annexe to our lounge where the large sliding doors opened onto the conservatory. Alan was resting on the comfy settee.
Sophie called through to Alan,

"Dad, I'm going now. I thought you might like to see me in my eighties' clothes."

Alan was acting in a really strange manner, shaking and unable to speak. Sophie called to me in a very worried tone,

"Mum, come quick, I think there's something wrong with dad."

As I arrived next to Sophie and looked into the conservatory, I knew there was a problem. I ran through the open door, trying to make sense of what was happening. He could not talk, only stare – deep down I knew he was going to leave us.

I ran to get Wendy, Sophie's carer. I telephoned James, who arrived in minutes. I just could not go back into the conservatory, but Wendy and James did all they could to try to save his life until the emergency team arrived and took over. My dearest Alan was going to leave us.

While all this was going on, Sophie texted Jay:

"Really sorry, I'm not going to make it tonight. Dad's just arrested. Paramedics are working on him now."

This news somehow reached my good friend, Chrissie, who was at the MICA for the event. She must have left immediately, as she turned up while Alan was still in the hands of the paramedics.

Stephen Rice, who was the island's lay preacher and a very good friend of our family, said a special prayer, surrounded by all of us. Sophie and I remained in the sitting room, feeling too emotional at the time to say our farewells.

Because it was a sudden and unexplained death, the police arrived and had to remain until the undertakers came to take Alan away.

The whole family was absolutely devastated at the loss of Alan. It was a terrible shock to lose such a loving husband, dad, grandad and great-grandad. He was always there for us all and would be greatly missed.

* * *

Alan's funeral had been arranged to take place at West Mersea Church on Tuesday the 27th of February 2018, at twelve noon, and would be conducted by Reverend Brian Snelling and Stephen Rice.

Kim and Vicky really wanted their dad to take his last journey in a horse-drawn carriage, although it was going to cost over a thousand pounds more than a car would be. However, we all opted for the horses. I don't think Alan would have chosen the dearest option.

For some days before the funeral, there were strong winds and heavy snow. Some roads had been closed and traffic diverted. The day before the funeral, we were informed that it would be too dangerous to use the horse-drawn carriage and a funeral car would have to be used instead. We were half expecting this to happen, so it wasn't a big surprise.

Members of the church realised from various conversations they had heard that there was going to be a lot of people at the funeral and it was possible that there may not be enough room inside. They organised for speakers to be put up in the churchyard so that people could still hear the service outside.

James and Maggie had organised for a large awning and heater to be put up outside the Art Café, opposite the church. This is where we would all be returning to after the funeral and there was a concern that the café might not be big enough to take all the mourners.

There was a large gathering of friends and relations inside and outside our house in Rosebank Road. It was a big surprise to see so many of the children we had fostered over the years, now all adults. I think they had seen the announcement in the newspaper.

We all began to make our way outside the house ready for the funeral cars to turn up, headed by the hearse carrying Alan. Sadly, there was no horse-drawn carriage, as it was too big a risk with the heavy snow. The route that was taken to the church was down Victory Road, then left onto Coast Road, past the houseboats. A lot of the followers were walking. As we passed one of the snow-lined slopes, Stephen Rice had written large words in the snow – BYE AL. It was very emotional seeing those words.

Arriving at the church, Alan's coffin was carried in by Kim and Chloe, Vicky and Charlotte, then George and Debbie Dawson.

The family all put a lot of loving thought into arranging the funeral service, with help from Stephen, who was part of the church service. To begin, James and his friend Peter Banks played their musical instruments and sang a beautiful song called I'll Fly Away. Then, Sophie paid tribute with some lovely words. Next, Alan's brother (Mick) and his wife (Mo), both musicians, played and sang the song, Will The Circle Be Unbroken. Stephen read Pixie's Words, followed by a Bible reading (John, Chapter 14, verses 1-6) and the eulogy, which had been written by the family. Following this were some lovely words read by Will. Vicky asked Stephen to read a poem titled Dad, written by Judy Burnett. We chose the hymns Sing Hosanna and All Things Bright and Beautiful. After a lovely service, the exit music played – This Train, by Big Bill Broonzy, then Happiness, by Ken Dodd.

After laying Alan to rest at Firs Road Cemetery, everyone returned to the Art Café where happy memories were recalled. It was remembered that Alan was very kind and generous, but that he was also careful with money, especially when shopping for groceries. He would always work out which was the cheapest brand before putting it in the basket, whereas I would opt for the best known names. There were times when my choice would be put back on the shelf and exchanged for something cheaper, and it probably tasted exactly the same! The comments went on to say that Alan would have been delighted with the heavy snowfall which cancelled his journey in a horse-drawn carriage, as we saved well over a thousand pounds. The family, although disappointed at not being able to have the beautiful black horses, reckoned 'dear old Dad' had something to do with the bad weather and much laughter followed this suggestion.

CHAPTER 58

Saying goodbye to my beloved Alan was hard, but with all my family and friends around me, I managed to get through that difficult day. We all shared laughter as well as tears, which is what Al would have loved. I believe we gave him the day he deserved.

CHAPTER 59

Sassy Sophia

OVERLEAF: *Sophie with Lyn and Reg in Los Angeles.*
ABOVE: *(Top) Sophie, Lyn and Reg in San Francisco at the start of their journey; Sophie at the Grand Canyon at the end of her big adventure.*

Sophie had been saving for at least two years to go on her dream road trip in America. Her two travel companions were going to be Matthew Palmer (Reg) and his lovely partner, Lyn. We first met Reg when he was a policeman during the time we were fostering teenagers and he became a really good friend of the family.

Sophie's much anticipated trip finally started on Friday the 1st of June at 8:30am, when her home carer packed all her luggage and wheelchair into the car, ready to leave Mersea and meet up with Reg and Lyn in Colchester. Reg was then going to drive his own car to the airport. I just had to take the journey to Colchester to say a fond good luck and farewell to them all, before returning back home again with Sophie's carer.

I was suddenly missing Alan, as he usually drove Sophie and her carer direct to the airport on occasions when she was going abroad. I always went along with them, as I enjoyed the journey and the views of the countryside. I expect Sophie was also quietly missing her dad. She was so lucky to have Reg and Lyn as companions on this huge adventure.

All went to plan once they arrived at Heathrow, with the assistance onto the plane and the onboard wheelchair being available to get Sophie to the toilet if needed. They actually took off at 2:15pm and, after eleven hours, arrived in San Francisco at 5:20pm. The eight-hour time difference made them feel strange, especially when their bodies were still on the UK time of 1:15am. You really need to push on through for five hours in this situation, and push on through is what they did!

After arriving at San Francisco airport, the first sigh of relief for Sophie was seeing her wheelchair again after the eleven hour flight. It was like seeing an old friend. The minute she sat back in it, she felt comfortable again. Next stop was the hotel via wheelchair accessible taxi, fairly readily available at the airport and in most cities. The Sir Francis Drake Hotel was a nice, Art Deco-style hotel, not far from Union Square.

It was early evening, so they decided to go for a stroll. They soon came across the financial district, then a somewhat unlit and seedy China Town. Not sure where this was leading, they decided to head back to somewhere more inviting. Stumbling across the Union Square Sports Bar, which wasn't all that far from the hotel, they ventured inside. People were very friendly and the barmaid even made Sophie her own cocktail. They named it 'Sassy Sophia' and this wasn't the last of a persona within Sophie that had been dying to come out.

Day two started with a good old American-style fry-up, a hearty breakfast that would see them through most of the day. They then set off to explore San Francisco on foot. This wasn't easy, with some of the incredibly steep hills – it really is like you see in the movies. But Reg was determined that they would be able to manage, and they did. Eventually, they made it down to the port area, finding the famous Fisherman's Wharf and the different pier areas, all very vibrant and buzzing. At Pier 33, they found the boarding point for a trip on the ferry to Alcatraz, all wheelchair accessible. Even Alcatraz itself was very well set up for wheelchair access.

Everyone takes the same audio tour and Sophie was able to access it all. It was all very intimidating, standing in the actual cells at times, with the tour revealing the grim history of its inmates, tales of escapes and attempted escapes. Interestingly though, staff and their families lived on the island and it was considered to be a close community. It even had gardens and play areas for the children. Overall, it was a haunting, sobering tour, but so worth doing.

CHAPTER 59

Day three was all about the helicopter tour of San Francisco. Sophie had done helicopter tours before in New York, so knew it should be possible, but she was still worried about whether Reg would be able to get her into the helicopter. It was absolutely fine though. The minute they took off, she couldn't take the smile off her face. The tour took them over the whole city. Knowing that this was part of Sophie's 'big birthday' trip, the pilot treated them not only to flying over The Golden Gate Bridge, but then also back under it. It took a while to come back down to earth afterwards! A long walk back from the bridge to the city certainly did the trick though. Along the coastal pathway there were long stretches of beach, which they hadn't realised would be part of the San Francisco experience.

Their last evening in San Francisco took them to The Swig Bar, which had a blues jam session. Sophie had taken her harmonicas, just in case such an opportunity arose. She introduced herself to the host, Ed, who was very enthused by the idea of her playing with the house band. He told her she would be in good company, with four or five other harmonica players. Sophie gulped. It was too late to back down though. When it came to her spot, she took a few deep breaths and went for it. She did okay and the crowd really liked her. As she got into that performance zone, she was at ease. The crowd whooped and the band urged her on. As her spot came to an end, she was on a high, but relieved that she did more than just hold her own. A great way to end the San Francisco leg of the journey!

On day four, after hiring a car, Reg drove them down to Monterey along the Pacific Coast Highway 1, giving them their first spectacular glimpse of the coastal drive. At every turn there was another breathtaking view of the Pacific Ocean and the various shorelines – long stretches of beach, intermingled with high rock formations. Their hotel, The Monterey Tides, certainly lived up to its name. Right on the beach, they could almost feel the Pacific waves as they sat watching the sea, talking of their planned whale watching trip the next day. Suddenly, they saw a vertical spout of water in the distance. A whale spouted as it rose and then dived again! This was boding well for the next day.

They got up early on day five and took a twenty-minute drive down to Moss Landing for the whale watching trip. Their marine biologist guide, Drake, excitedly reported that they had seen whales on the earlier trip that morning. Heading out of the harbour, they saw some sea otters basking on their backs. Just out of the harbour, Drake shouted that he could see a pod of humpbacked whales. Everyone rushed to the side of the boat and sure enough they could be seen a little further out. They rose out of the water briefly, allowing a fleeting glimpse and some ideal photo opportunities. It happened so quickly that most pictures just captured the tail as they dived again. It was so thrilling.

Drake then announced that some great white sharks had been seen about an hour away, so they headed further out. As they got near the sighting area, Drake's enthusiastic commentary let them know he had spotted one. Sophie was excited, but also slightly nervous, as all she could think about was the film Jaws! As they got closer, people could be seen on the beach in the distance, as well as people swimming. Sophie said she wanted to shout out like in the film, "Get out of the water!", but obviously she remained silent. Then, suddenly, one of the sharks was right with them. It was breathtaking seeing it basking in the water alongside the boat. After several more sightings, it was time to head back.

Unfortunately, during the shark spotting, in a brief lapse of concentration, Sophie dropped her mobile phone. It hit the deck and promptly slid straight through the vent in the side of the boat and into the ocean. She was absolutely gutted as she saw it sinking in slow motion. She thought at least it was only her phone and not herself sinking to a watery grave in the

CHAPTER 59

Pacific. The day of whales and sharks was worth it.

On day six, the next destination was Pismo Beach and another great drive for Reg along the stunning Pacific coast. The drive was rather longer than expected, with detours because of roadworks and a fire. The hotel was another lovely beach hotel, although it had a slightly more Ibiza-style feel than the breathtaking Monterey. There wasn't much here apart from hotels and a few shops, so they decided to relax for a while, before getting an evening meal at the nearby bar and restaurant. The shrimp choice was delicious, with shrimps the size of king prawns! This echoed most dining experiences – big on size.

On day seven, they were on the road again, this time to Santa Barbara, where they met a friend of a friend for lunch and a personally guided tour. Jill met them in the lobby of the rather luxurious Hilton Hotel, right on the seafront promenade. Santa Barbara is known for being rather an exclusive place where certain celebrities have homes – Oprah Winfrey and Ellen de Generes among them. The previous January, there had been an awful mudslide, with twenty-two deaths and quite a few homes lost. Their lovely guide took them up to the area where it had happened. Despite being six months ago, the devastation was still clear, with remains of houses and some huge boulders that came down with the mudslide. It showed that wealth does not protect anyone from the power of nature.

After that very sobering experience, they saw some of the old town including The Court House, which is still used today for sentencing. Much of the architecture there is based around the very pretty Mediterranean style. The town is also notable for its flowers and greenery. Wherever they walked, they were not far from fragrant flowers. Everyone agreed they could have easily stayed longer. However, a Los Angeles weekend awaited.

Day eight was to be the last bit of coastline driving for Reg. They now headed down to Santa Monica. Along the way, he drove through Malibu, reportedly an area for the rich and famous with their houses overlooking the beach and ocean. Disappointingly, all they seemed to pass on the road through was more like the backs of chalet-type homes and the backs of Ibiza-style apartment blocks.

Sophie said that, for her, Santa Monica was much more the place to hang out, which is exactly what they did for a couple of hours before the drive to LA itself. They strolled along the long, wide promenade right on the beach edge. The beach itself went out for miles before hitting the sea. People rode along the promenade on skateboards, bikes and electric scooters, which seemed to have taken over from roller skates. The famous Santa Monica pier, with its roller coaster and other rides, was a hive of activity, with musicians and artists spread out along its length.

After a couple of hours in the blistering heat, they were ready for an icy slush drink and the air-conditioned drive to LA. The journey, which they expected to take an hour, ended up taking nearly two hours because of traffic delays and a slight map mishap. However, they got a greater view of this sprawling city that was less high-rise. Once they found the hotel, just off Hollywood Boulevard, they knew they had arrived. The view from the hotel window of the Hollywood Hills, and the infamous Hollywood sign, confirmed it.

Days nine to eleven were spent in Los Angeles. Their first full day there was packed with activity. They did two tours, both very different. The first, and by far the best, was a tour of Warner Brothers Studios, one of the big names in movie making. Getting to see around the 'backlots,' the exterior sets and street scenes was incredible. Numerous legends had trodden these 'streets', from actors in the 1930s/40s to those still making films today. Of course, it's all fake. It's all made of plaster, no bricks, to enable easy changes of facades when explosions are part of the plot. Then, there were the studios themselves, taking in the Big Bang Theory set and the iconic Friends set with the Central Perk Café, where sitting on the

CHAPTER 59

famous sofa is obligatory.

Next, was a tour of movie stars' homes. It was fascinating to glimpse a view of the former or current homes of celebrities like Michael Jackson, Elvis (before his move to Graceland), Al Pacino, Quentin Tarantino, Katy Perry and Rod Stewart. They also drove along Rodeo Drive, known for its high-class shops and the scenes from the film Pretty Woman, where Julia Roberts had a bit of trouble clothes shopping. At the end of Rodeo Drive was the Beverly Wilshire Hotel, also from Pretty Woman. Sophie was determined to go back there the next day. But the evening was to be more of the Hollywood showbiz mania.

They walked down Hollywood Boulevard, part of the Walk of Fame with the stars embedded into the pavement. Actors dressed as Wonder Woman, characters from Star Wars and the like, all offered photo opportunities. Their evening meal was at a quirky restaurant called The Beetle House – a Tim Burton themed place, with actors dressed as his movie characters to lure you in. Sophie was taken with Edward Scissorhands and Johnny Depp's Willy Wonka, who, finding out it was her birthday trip, indulged them in conversation during their meal. Not once did he venture out of character. Another cocktail, a staple part of the trip now, was definitely appropriate here. It came in the form of a Drink Your Dessert cocktail.

The following day was a leisurely Sunday. They headed down to Santa Monica Boulevard, having heard there was to be a large LA Pride parade. Thousands were anticipated and indeed there must have been thousands in the parade alone. It was extremely colourful with lashings of flamboyant characters and costumes; a real carnival atmosphere. After three hours and with the parade still in progress, they decided to leave.

Their next stop was Rodeo Drive. This time they walked along doing some window shopping before arriving at Sophie's intended destination, The Beverly Wilshire Hotel. She knew they couldn't afford a meal there, but her research showed a cocktail would be within reach. Before that though, she had a cheeky chat with the concierge and before she knew it she was being taken up in the elevator to view a penthouse suite, similar to the one in Pretty Woman. It turned out that some scenes were actually shot in this very suite - The Presidential Suite, no less! - including that balcony scene when she leans back over the balcony.

Sophie had to pinch herself to believe she was there. The only way for her to finish off this visit was with that cocktail that she had promised herself. It just had to be the Pretty Woman – an exquisitely light, fizzy mix of champagne, vodka, raspberries and rose petal. Sophie's movie experience and the tastes of the high life in LA were unforgettable. And the trip was not yet over…

Leaving Los Angeles on day eleven, they took a trip up to the Griffith Observatory for one last look at the city. From this impressive vantage point, you could see the sprawling city on one side and the Hollywood sign on the other. With no time to dwell on what had been a truly Hollywood experience, they set off on their longest journey yet: to Las Vegas, four hours away. The further inland they drove, the hotter it became.

The first stop was worth getting out into the scorching sun for – the Hoover Dam. At any point you would find people looking over the edge of the concrete wall on the road across the dam. Unfortunately, Sophie wasn't tall enough in her wheelchair to see over the wall. So, what did her very able companion Reg do? He lifted her up and tilted her slightly to view over the wall. Her heart was in her mouth as she said,

"I can see it! Enough! You can put me down now!"

It was a breathtaking moment. It was also one of the rare moments of disappointment regarding accessibility. Why were there no areas with railings? At least she would have been able to see through railings. A guide gave them a top tip though, saying that the best view would be from the walkway on the Memorial Bridge as they headed out. It was a view

CHAPTER 59

from a distance of one thousand feet above ground, but it was spectacular to see the enormity of the dam from there and with no worries about being dropped over the wall! Before expiring in the incredible hundred-degree heat, they continued for a further three hours to Las Vegas.

Days eleven to thirteen were spent in Las Vegas. They realised just how 'middle of the desert' Vegas was when they had driven through vast areas seeing little else. Suddenly, out of nowhere there was a cityscape of high and low-rise buildings. Finding the New York New York hotel on the famous Vegas Strip, Reg parked up and went into the lobby to check in. It was enormous, like no other lobby they had been in. Where lobby ended and casino or shopping mall began, was indistinguishable. Much of the experience of Vegas revolves around meandering through different hotels, where each is a different spectacle of flamboyance, shopping opportunities and gambling temptations. Almost every hotel had its own casino. So, Sophie decided to give roulette a go. Sitting on the stool at the high table like a pro, she spread the chips over the possible winning numbers. She lost and she won, but came out on top enough to buy a new watch with the winnings.

They then visited two iconic hotels, Caesars Palace and the Bellagio. The renowned Bellagio Fountains display in front of the hotel was spectacular, as was the plush interior and shops. Equally lavish were the interiors of Caesars Palace, with its shopping malls in the style of Italian streets. Above, was a skyscape of an evening summer sky, making you feel like you really were outside. Here, Sophie suddenly had a 'Sassy Sophia' moment as she went into Cartier. Without going into details, she ended up wearing a $17,000 necklace. Naturally, it looked beautiful on her, but, of course, it had to go back into its cabinet. Sophie said she felt like a million dollars just for a few moments. Typically, it was another reminder of the sinkhole for money that Vegas is.

Days thirteen to fifteen were spent in The Grand Canyon,

the original point to the trip and the thing that Sophie had always wanted to do. As they headed into the Grand Canyon National Park, it already felt so different from the cities and coastal adventures. In the wooded lodgings area, everything was so much more rustic and closer to nature. So close, in fact, that deer would just wander around at all times of the day! Arriving just before evening, they just relaxed with pizza and beer from the on-site supermarket, watching out for deer.

The following morning was the big day – the helicopter trip over the canyon. Sophie could barely contain her excitement as the helicopter took off. Six minutes later, they went over the canyon rim. It was mind-blowing! As they went over the edge, it was like going off the edge of the world. It went down forever, a mile deep in places. What the eyes were seeing was difficult for the brain to comprehend. The vast depth below and ahead was indescribable. As if the helicopter trip wasn't enough, later that day, as they wandered around, they realised their lodge was just ten minutes from the rim. They could see it again from the ground. They waited for sundown and watched the sunset over the canyon. It was the perfect way to end the trip of all trips. With so many unforgettable experiences, it truly was the once in a lifetime trip Sophie had hoped for.

When people ask Sophie "What's next?", her response is,

"For now it's back to reality, earning a living and saving for whatever I dream up next."

I am sure Sophie still has plenty of dreams…

CHAPTER 59

SASSY SOPHIA

A broken heart and a new lease of life

OVERLEAF: *During an unusual Christmas Eve in 2020, some of the family outside on Pixie's doorstep for a socially distanced meet up before the country went into another lockdown.*
ABOVE: *(Top) St Bartholomew's Hospital, London; Pixie with Will's mother-in-law and close friend Jenny Hambly.*

Towards the end of 2019, around November, I had been feeling slightly breathless at times. I just thought it was stress-related because of the loss of Alan, although it had been over a year since he had died. These breathless moments did seem to start after his passing. However, there was one occasion when I struggled halfway up the stairs. On reaching the bedroom, I needed to lay on the floor, exhausted. I called downstairs and Abi, Sophie's carer, came and chatted with me until I calmed down and was able to breathe again.

After this scare, I was talked into having a medical check-up by the family, which led to an appointment being made for me to go to Harwich hospital for an echocardiogram the very next day. I was feeling very nervous, as I don't like hospitals. All seemed to be going alright until we went into the consulting room where I was told I had stenosis of the aortic valve, with the level of risk being severe. It meant that I would have to have an operation as soon as possible, and they would prefer me to go direct from Harwich to Colchester Hospital by ambulance. I put forward the argument that I wanted to go home first to collect all my clothes and toiletries, but I was told,

"In that case you will be travelling at your own risk and we can't be held responsible for your safety. If you feel unwell at all on the way home you must go straight to the hospital."

The journey from Harwich back to West Mersea was an emotionally difficult one, knowing what lay ahead. That evening I went into Colchester General Hospital where I spent the next ten weeks.

At last I had an appointment to visit St Bartholomew's Hospital in London – the world famous Barts – regarding the procedure known as TAVI to put my heart condition right. The ambulance arrived at Colchester General Hospital, where I had now been for six weeks, at 8:00am with two very helpful men: the driver, and the assistant for the rear of the ambulance to help me, if necessary. I sat in a comfortable upright seat, as did Spike, my caring and talkative helper, who lived in Harwich. Because of the time I had been in hospital, this journey to London was very enjoyable. I was comforted by the thought of being on the way to gaining my good health back again.

Today, I was going to have a pre-medical talk and various tests in preparation for the TAVI. We arrived at Barts as planned, just before 11:00am. Sophie and Kim travelled to London by train and arrived about fifteen minutes later. Their support was absolutely critical to me, especially at the interviews with the various medical professionals.

I had a few tests and a long chat explaining the TAVI procedure, which Sophie and Kim were present for. We were all able to ask questions, which was very helpful. Knowing what I had got ahead of me was very enlightening and in some ways a relief. It was possible that I could return home the day after the operation. I had initially been told three days. Unfortunately, I had a few hours to wait until the final part of the preparation work could be done.

At 4:10pm, I was called to the radiology department. This was where one of the most important parts of my treatment was to happen. Kim had already explained to me about the size of the equipment and said that in no way was it intrusive or claustrophobic and that it should give me no cause for worry or distress.

I sat in the wheelchair, clothed in a hospital gown, ready to

CHAPTER 60

be moved onto the narrow, but comfortable bed, which was adapted to slide into the huge doughnut-shaped scanner. All was well as I moved slowly towards the scanner, then my head entered – I suddenly panicked and shouted,

"I can't breathe, get me out!"

I was immediately withdrawn from the scanner – a shaking wreck, ashamed of myself for my reactions. I apologised to the kind man in charge of the whole operation. He assured me that the situation could be reversed and prepared me for another attempt. He even went to find Sophie and Kim, who were waiting in one of the rooms down the corridor.

When they appeared, I felt well supported and ready to have another go at entering the 'doughnut'. I lay down, as relaxed as I could possibly get, and was now moving into the hole. I looked up, and then sideways – I couldn't breathe.

"I can't breathe!" I shouted.

I was pulled out again. Every inch of my body was shaking, and I was close to tears. The young man in charge still did not get angry in any way, but then said,

"Pixie, there's no point in trying any more times because your mind won't be able to take in the breathing instructions that I'll be giving you. We'll give it a rest for today."

I returned to the single room, where I had left my clothes and we prepared for the journey back to Colchester in the ambulance. Sophie and Kim returned by train. It had been a long day.

There was a positive side to our visit to Barts. When we arrived, I was amazed at the beauty of the exterior of the buildings all around and during our long periods of waiting time, we were able to gather together some information regarding the hospital.

The first physician was appointed at St Bartholomew in 1562. Nurses, or Sister's Helpers were only mentioned in 1647. St Bartholomew's Hospital has provided continuous patient care in the same place for longer than any other hospital in England. In 2023, the hospital will celebrate its 900th anniversary. It was in 1995 that it became known as Barts. Because of the problems I had with my CT scan at Barts, it was agreed that I would be given the opportunity of another scan, which I knew I had to do – my life depended on the TAVI operation. Barts' medical staff then allowed Colchester hospital to perform the necessary CT scan within their facilities, reducing the waiting time considerably.

My terrifyingly short stay in hospital had now turned into a massive ten weeks. When was this all going to end? I had always had a fear of hospitals, together with being claustrophobic, an absolute nightmare to medical staff, who were a force to be proud of.

* * *

Each day during my stay in hospital began at 7am with a trip to the washroom, followed by getting dressed – I did not spend my day in bed. Breakfast next, and then I spent quite a lot of time writing in the television room. With all of the modern machines and medical treatments around me, I began to think back to some old-fashioned Mersea remedies, sayings, terms and superstitions. I'll start with some remedies.

Remedies

BEE AND WASP STINGS
Mix bicarbonate of soda with vinegar and put on the sting. You can rub on the mixture with half an onion if you have one at hand.

NOSE BLEEDS
My mother would always get the old-fashioned, large back door key and put it on my back under my clothes.

It really did work. The shock of the cold key probably had something to do with it.

SHOCK, OR PANIC
One tablespoon of whisky, one level teaspoon of sugar with a little hot water. This works wonders.

INDIGESTION
A quarter of a teaspoon of bicarbonate of soda in very hot water. Sip gently.

AN APPLE A DAY
Keeps the doctor away.

STINGING NETTLES
If you ever get stung by nettles, I guarantee that in the area close by there will be some dock leaves. Pick a leaf and hold it on the sting. You have a cure at hand. Strange, but true - it's nature's way of looking after you.

EXTRA SHINY HAIR
Do a final rinse with a jug of warm water containing a tablespoon of vinegar.

CRAMP
This is another unusual cure I can vouch for personally. It was passed on to Mum by the man who worked at Charles Brown's, the hardware store in East Street, Colchester. He came to the island on a regular basis, delivering oil for oil stoves and oil lamps. This memory goes back many years. He always had a cup of tea when calling at our house. On this occasion, mum suffered a bout of cramp. The 'oil man' offered a cure, talking in a broad Essex accent. I listened to what he had to say.

"Well, mate, when you go to bed at night, place your

shoes on the floor with one shoe facing one way, toe in front and the other shoe facing the other way with the heel at the front and toe at the back. If you do this when you go to bed, your cramp will go."

We all found this laughable, but discovered that it did work – how or why I do not know, but I used this method myself, and have passed it on to many friends over the years.

WARTS

Alan had a problem with warts on his hands. We had been told of a cure by an Irish man, using a full moon. I had to take part in this very weird cure. Firstly, we had to wait for a full moon. Then, when the moon was shining bright, I had to take off my gold wedding ring, let the moonbeam shine on my ring and rub it over the warts. I began to laugh and I said to Alan,

"I can't believe I'm doing this. I feel like a witch!"

After a short time had passed, we were all sitting round the dinner table and Alan shouted,

"Guess what? My warts have all disappeared!"

We all burst out laughing. The moon really does hold magic powers.

Old sayings, terms and superstitions

I was inspired to get my paints out (something I'd not done for many years) and have fun depicting some of these old sayings.

Seed growers on the island would choose the time of a full moon to plant their seeds, as the power of a full moon was equal to the sunshine during the day.

Never shed a clout til May is out – could mean don't start wearing summer clothes until the May blossom is out, as

May blossom doesn't bloom until the weather is warm enough. It could also be argued that it is just referring to the month of May.

Hind part afore – means back to front.

To come a right purler – means to fall over.

A BROKEN HEART AND A NEW LEASE OF LIFE

Someone may ask you "How many do you want?" and you might reply with a proper old Mersea saying, *"The best part of a tidy few."*

Someone very mean would be – *as tight as a duck's arse under water.*

CHAPTER 60

Rain sayings:
>*Rain before seven, fine before eleven.*
>*Rain from the east, two hours at least.*
>*Rain on the ebb, go home to bed.*

A bandy legged person couldn't stop a pig in a passage – meaning it would run straight through the person's legs.

A very thin person would be – *as thin as a yard of pump water.*

The next saying comes from the watermen, possibly teaching boys to work on the water:
>*One boy is equal to one boy*
>*Two boys are equal to half a boy*
>*Three boys are equal to no boy at all*

This one is something I would hear by my Uncle Les Clarke:
   As a bird is known for his feathers,
   a man is known for his conversation.

If something's not quite
straight, it's – *on the huh.*

CHAPTER 60

Shitehawk – the Mersea nickname for a seagull.

A snail is known
as a – *Hobneydod.*

A BROKEN HEART AND A NEW LEASE OF LIFE

And finally…

*There's a little bit of good in the worst of us
and a little bit of bad in the best of us.*

There are many more sayings that could be mentioned and I am sure anyone reading through this chapter could think of more. I have just written some that came into my mind. Hopefully, when some of 'us oldens' have moved into the heavenly realms, a few old words and sayings will still be remembered.

* * *

During those ten weeks in hospital, the world changed.
There began to be talk of a new, deadly virus, Covid-19, or Coronavirus. For most of my stay in hospital everything seemed fairly normal, but the outside world was changing. As the weeks went on, we all had to take extra care over hand sanitising to

prevent the spread of all viruses, but especially this new one. As the virus spread, it was becoming a pandemic. In the last couple of weeks of my stay in hospital, it became more noticeable how side rooms were being closed off. Despite the concerns of my family, the staff reassured us not to be too concerned.

I had a lot of respect for the nursing staff and also for Doctor Ioannis Kounturas, a Greek doctor, who actually studied and became a doctor in Greece. He was always ready to answer my numerous questions during my ten weeks in Colchester.

On the 17th of March 2020, I was approached by Doctor Ioannis saying that an ambulance would be taking me to Barts the next day, the 18th of March, for the long-awaited TAVI heart procedure. The whole family were in a frantic panic after hearing the news that the operation was imminent. Sophie and Kim had promised to support me by being in London, travelling by train and staying at a Travelodge close to the hospital. It was such a relief for me to have the girls close to me, especially at a time when London was now showing the effects of the worldwide Coronavirus pandemic.

The ambulance journey for me was weird, with hardly any traffic on the roads. Little did I know of the experience that Kim, Sophie, and her carer, Wendy, were having travelling by train. They told of Liverpool Street Station, usually always extremely busy, being largely deserted when they got off the practically empty train. It felt unnerving, almost ghostly. Everything was coming to a standstill.

When we arrived at Barts, it was all systems go! Preparation work began immediately for my operation. There was no doubt it would be all over today and I would hopefully return the next day, if all went to plan.

We were so lucky as everything did go to plan. I was taken to what was called the operating lab – the room where the operation took place. I was then taken back to the ward at least two hours later.

While they were waiting, Sophie and Kim went to the

courtyard, wandered round and found the hospital Church of Saint Bartholomew the Less. It was here that they said a prayer to bring me through the operation. Their prayers were answered. I stayed overnight and returned to Mersea by car the next day.

Although I was driven to Barts by ambulance, there was nothing available for the return journey. My return would be by car, driven by Andy and accompanied by my grandson, Dudley. Kim had stayed in London to be at the hospital with me, ready to get me outside to the car. Everywhere was chaotic, with a shortage of staff. London was like a ghost town, with only a few lights on in the few shops that were open – a sight I hope we never see again. At least there were no hold-ups on the way home.

We were lucky to be back on Mersea Island, safe and sound. After ten weeks away from home, stepping through the front door made me realise how much I had missed everything. There was also an emotional memory of the time I left Colchester Hospital to make the journey to the Acute Cardiac Ward. The ambulance men pushed me in a wheelchair along the wide corridor, lined with doctors and nurses giving me a wonderful 'good luck' cheer that stayed with me all the way - thanks to God, universal love and my family.

It was just a few days later that the country went into its first lockdown, something none of us had ever experienced before. If I hadn't been taken to Barts when I was, things might have been a very different story for me. I was so lucky to be given a new lease of life, one which meant I could complete these memoirs, and hopefully create new memories and stories for years to come.

CHAPTER 60

A BROKEN HEART AND A NEW LEASE OF LIFE